Measure
Your Life

Measure Your Life

17 Ways to Evaluate Your Life from God's Perspective

Wesley L. Duewel

ZondervanPublishingHouse

Academic and Professional Books

Grand Rapids, Michigan

A Division of HarperCollinsPublishers

Measure Your Life
Copyright © 1992 by Wesley L. Duewel

Requests for information should be addressed to:
Zondervan Publishing House
Academic and Professional Books
Grand Rapids, Michigan 49530

Library of Congress Cataloging-in-Publication Data

Duewel, Wesley L.
   Measure your life / Wesley L. Duewel.
     p.   cm.
   Includes indexes.
   ISBN 0-310-54781-4
   1. Christian life–1960- I. Title.
BV4501.2.D738 1992
248.4.–dc20   91-34044
                                         CIP

Edited by Robert D. Wood
Cover designed by Jamison Bell

Printed in the United States of America

92 93 94 95 96 / AM / 10 9 8 7 6 5 4 3 2 1

CONTENTS

FOREWORD

In the race of life, anybody can win the first hundred yards. It's an exceptional person, indwelt by the living Christ and filled with the Holy Spirit, who finishes the race well.

When Olympic runner Eric Liddell refused to compete on Sunday because it was the Lord's Day, he was measuring his life from the perspective of the ultimate finish line—when he would stand before his Savior—not when he would stand before photographers with an Olympic medal around his neck.

I consider myself very fortunate that my parents, spiritual mentors, and the Lord have taught me to measure my life, to make decisions while keeping in mind the end of the race, not the first hundred yards. I can't count the number of times that this perspective has kept me from compromising God's best for what would have been merely mediocre or, much worse, sin.

Thus, my delight to recommend to you Dr. Wesley Duewel's book *Measure Your Life*. I've had the privilege of knowing Dr. Duewel for many years now and can say with absolute confidence that he has run to win!

In this book, Dr. Duewel presents the twenty-one criteria by which he has measured and lived out his life. Although he illustrates his points with rich stories about some of God's most distinguished servants, there's no question but that each compelling statement he makes has been borne out of his own experience many times over.

Wesley Duewel is a highly respected missionary statesman and a man of unusual spiritual stature, someone who has been running the Christian race with his eye on the prize. I admire that kind of persistence! And I thank God to know that he's been touching the world by his prayers for me and for so many others all these years.

Here is a book worth grabbing hold of, written by a man worth following. Ask God to begin using Dr. Duewel's words to encourage and challenge you today. The rewards of a measured, Christlike life will be eternal.

Dr. Luis Palau, President
Luis Palau Evangelistic Association

1

GOD IS EAGER
TO REWARD YOU

D o you realize that God is planning tremendous rewards for you? No matter how wonderful your understanding of God is, you have never begun even to realize how good God is. Nor do you fully realize how personally He loves you. Most likely you have never even dreamed what a joy it is for God to see you do His will, to feel your love to Him, and to plan the good things He wants you to share when you reach the home He is preparing for you to share with Him in heaven.

It is always a joy to plan a surprise for someone you love. God has created us with capacity for that kind of joy because He Himself has known such joy from all eternity. He loves to plan. When He showed the angels the earth He had been planning, they shouted their joy in heavenly enthusiasm (Job 38:7). But the joy God had in planning the earth is far less than His joy as He now makes plans for you in heaven and your life there.

It is a tremendous joy to God that you and others who love Him will be able to share with Him all that His love is planning for you forever and ever and ever! He is so delighted, so thrilled, so expectant. He has only given you hints of all the delightful surprises He is planning.

Jesus shares that holy joy and excited heavenly anticipation! Don't you remember what He promised? "I will prepare a place for you. We are going to be there together forever. I will come and take you there to be with me" (John 14:1–3). No doubt Jesus' heart often calls to you, "Oh, if you only could realize all the joy that I am planning for you!"

I was in Japan for the eightieth anniversary of the denomination that grew out of the ministry of OMS International. It was my joy to give the closing message, and I was requested to give a missionary challenge. One of the Japanese leaders gave the invitation. First, he asked those making first-time commitments to stand while he prayed for them. Then he asked the Christians who *knew* they were children of God and who longed to make a total surrender of their lives and their all for time and eternity and trust God for a mighty infilling of His Spirit to come and stand in front before the platform. Many, many gathered there.

Then he asked for those who would offer their lives for full-time missionary service in other lands to come. From all over the large auditorium in downtown Tokyo they came. They came down from the first balcony. They came down from the second balcony. I saw one youth start from the second balcony and run down the back steps. By the time he reached the main floor he began to run for fear he would not reach the platform in time. He almost leaped up the steps so eager was he to join the scores of others. My eyes filled with tears. How little did Charles Cowman dream of such a scene when he landed in Japan in 1901 to begin the ministry of OMS. What joy he will reap in heaven for planning and pouring out his life for souls in Japan.

Then four young leaders of another wonderful evangelical denomination, which is also an outgrowth of the work founded by Charles Cowman, met me at the close of the service and took me to a dining room high in one of the skyscrapers. They seemed so full of joy and love. They ordered food, and soon it began to come. One course followed another of delicious Japanese gourmet food. I began to say, "What, another course?" They just laughed for joy. And then here came another course. I finally lost count, but I must have tasted samples from at least seventeen delicious dishes.

I could see the love and joy in their faces as we shared fellowship together. Never have I seen anyone so thrilled to see their plan unfold for me. It was their excited joy to surprise me with one delight after another as several hours slipped by. Late that night one of them escorted me across Tokyo back to the OMS seminary campus.

That is only a faint picture of the joy Christ will radiate when in eternity He delights you with one holy, joyous reward after another. Not just for a few passing hours—it will continue forever. There will be new, ever more beautiful, ever more wonderful holy surprises through the unending ages of eternity. Why? Because God's love and grace have planned to delight you, bless you, surprise you, and reward you for ever and ever. If you could only fathom the indescribable joy of that reaping, you would make your greatest ambition today to sow in every possible way for eternity.

THINK OF THE AMAZING PLANS OF GOD

Human beings were created to be able to plan. Scientists have only begun to understand the amazing capacity of the human mind. But our minds realize only a fraction of their potential! If Adam and Eve had never

sinned, what amazing developments the people of this
world would share by now!

God shared with us the ability to be creative and to
plan, because He loves us so. He is the infinite Creator.
He is the Supreme Planner. What is God planning for
today? His greatest plans are not how to coordinate things
on earth. His greatest plans are for the wonderful future.
Everything that is related to our world today is tempo-
rary; eternity's plans are forever.

Listen to this! " 'I know the plans I have for you,' "
declares the LORD, " 'plans to prosper you . . . plans to
give you hope and a future' " (Jer. 29:11). "Many, O
LORD my God, are the wonders you have done. The
things you planned for us no one can recount to you; were
I to speak and tell of them, they would be too many to
declare" (Ps. 40:5). The good things God has already done
are but a small beginning token of all He plans to do for
us. "As the heavens are higher than the earth, so are my
ways higher than your ways and my thoughts than your
thoughts" (Isa. 55:9). "No eye has seen, no ear has heard,
no mind has conceived what God has prepared for those
who love him" (1 Cor. 2:9). God is trying to say to you
and me, "Oh! If you only knew all the joys, the
experiences, the rewards I am planning for you!"

BEYOND ALL YOUR DREAMS

"Behold, I will create new heavens and a new earth.
The former things will not be remembered, nor will they
come to mind. But be glad and rejoice forever in what I
create. . . . I will rejoice . . . and take delight in my
people" (Isa. 65:17–19).

The future rewards God plans for you will be so
amazing, so blessedly fulfilling, so satisfying that you will
forget all the problems, trials, and the disappointments of

your life today. It will be worth every effort you have ever expended, every pressure you have ever endured, every price you ever paid to obey God and choose His highest will.

God will never be in debt to anyone. He will reward above and beyond what we could ever expect or deserve. This will be His great joy—to lavish joy and reward on you. "Our light and momentary troubles are achieving for us an eternal glory that far outweighs them all" (2 Cor. 4:17). We may experience weeping at times during earth's night. But eternal joy comes in God's great morning (Ps. 30:5).

"Our present sufferings are not worth comparing with the glory that will be revealed in us. The creation waits in eager expectation for the sons of God to be revealed" (Rom. 8:18–19). All creation seems expectant for God's great plans for us. Think how the angels can hardly wait for God to unveil all He has been planning for you and me. We are going to share it all when that glory is revealed (1 Peter 5:1). Peter speaks of this great reward in heaven as "the salvation that is ready to be revealed in the last time" (1 Peter 1:5). Our faith and faithfulness now will "result in praise, glory, and honor when Jesus Christ is revealed" (1 Peter 1:7).

YOUR REWARD DEMANDS ETERNITY

It will take all of eternity to experience all God is planning for you. Even so, the glory and extent of reward God will give you is dependent on how you live your life today. Reward is according to life. Reward is above and beyond anything we could ever conceive or desire. But reward is according to life. How you live today to some extent sets limits on all God will gladly give you in reward. You will reap above and beyond all you sow, but you will reap *according* to what you sow.

This fact makes it so important to understand the role of the way we live. It also makes it important that we measure our life according to the same measurements God uses. What is your life?

Life Is Made of Brevity

Life is made of brevity!
    Briefest years and weeks and days
Hours and minutes cross our ways.
    Once we greet them, then they flee—
Gone for all eternity.
    Life is made of brevity!

Life is made of little things!
    Opportunities—like seeds—
Harvests yield to him who heeds.
    Every fleeting brief minute
Has eternity in it.
    Life is made of little things!

Life is made of constant choice!
    Daily choices seem so small,
But our God records them all.
    Everything done for the Lord
Brings eternally reward.
    Life is made of constant choice!

Nothing in your life is small!
    All is opportunity
To sow for eternity.
    All you do has worth untold—
Life is reaped a millionfold!
    Nothing in your life is small!

Life for God cannot be lost!
    All you do for God today
As you labor, give, and pray
    You invest on heaven's shore;
You will reap it evermore!
    Life for God cannot be lost!

Wesley Duewel

2
YOUR LIFE IS GOD'S GIFT

Your life is God's good gift to you. No matter how difficult your circumstances, your life has far more potential than you have ever realized. Your life has only begun. It is your great opportunity. It is yours to invest or to spend. You can do more significant things with your life than you have ever realized, and this book is written to help you make a wise investment of it. No matter what your age, it is never too late to start planning and investing for eternity.

You were created for life. In fact, it is impossible for you to cease to exist. Once created, no human being can escape existence. The question is, Will it be only existence? Or, will it be life in the fullest, most wonderful sense of that term? It is not merely a question of heaven or hell. It is a question of all that heaven can include for you. The Bible points to great differences in the rewards of heaven. More than you have realized, your future reward is in your own hands. Your daily choices have eternal consequences, and God does not choose for you. You yourself must choose wisely.

GOD HAS A WONDERFUL PLAN FOR YOU

Jesus came that you might have life in its most wonderful sense, "and have it to the full" (John 10:10). No matter how good your life is, Jesus wants to make it better. No matter how satisfying it has been thus far, Jesus wants to make your future far more satisfying. God always has tremendous plans for you. Let me remind you again: "'I know the plans I have for you,' declares the LORD, 'plans to prosper you and not to harm you, plans to give you hope and a future. Then you will call upon me and come and pray to me, and I will listen to you. You will seek me and find me when you seek me with all your heart. I will be found by you,' declares the LORD" (Jer. 29:11–14).

As surely as God is in heaven, He has better plans for you tomorrow than you have ever realized thus far. The question is this: Will you use your today so that your tomorrow can be the greatest possible? Will you make the right decisions and use your life today so God can carry out His full plans for your tomorrows?

YOUR LIFE HAS ONLY BEGUN

Your life on earth, no matter how long, is only the tiniest part of your existence, which will never end. For every day you spend on earth, there will be billions and billions and billions of future years. In all of them, you will be reaping what you are sowing now. You cannot escape sowing, and you cannot escape reaping.

No matter now wonderful or how difficult your life is today, you can, if you will, prepare today for a better future. Life, whether you invest it or waste it, is future oriented. Your future is coming. It is on the way. Each day you are shaping its possibilities. You cannot postpone it. It cannot be escaped. Life for you has only begun. It will continue forever and ever.

YOUR LIFE IS CREATED FOR CHOICE

Life was created for choices. That means life was created to prepare for eternity. Eternity is coming; everyone is en route to eternity. You are today one day nearer. And each day you are making choices that will affect your eternity. The ability to choose is a Godlike gift. This makes character possible and, hence, the possibility of the gracious rewards God promises us if we live for Him and serve Him. Every right choice, everything you do to please and love God, to serve God, or to bless others adds to your eternal reward. Eternity is God's plan, place, and time for your ultimate and unending reward.

HEAVEN CONTAINS YOUR RECORD

God has planned for a comprehensive, complete, and perfect record of your life. No record kept by anyone in this world is nearly so complete as God's record. Undoubtedly the angels keep God's records. The watchers of Daniel 4:17 (in the Hebrew language) are the angels. No Christian is ever alone; God's angels are always near (Matt. 18:10; Ps. 34:7; Heb. 1:14). They are not only available to help you, but they are God's record keepers. How thrilled the angels are for every item they can place in your record that will add to your reward!

Heaven contains the Lamb's Book of Life, with the name of every believer. This is mentioned at least eight times in Scripture (Ex. 32:32–33; Ps. 69:28; Dan. 12:1; Luke 10:20; Phil. 4:3; Rev. 20:12; 21:27). There are also other books that contain the complete record of every life

(Ps. 87:6; Dan. 7:10; Rev. 20:12). "Then those who feared
the LORD talked with each other, and the LORD listened
and heard. A scroll of remembrance was written in his
presence concerning those who feared the LORD and
honored his name. 'They will be mine,' says the LORD
Almighty, 'in the day when I make up my treasured
possession. . . . You will again see the distinction between
the righteous and the wicked, between those who serve
God and those who do not'" (Mal. 3:16–18).

What are the kinds of things that are recorded in your
record in heaven? Scripture gives many suggestions:

Your whole life.	Romans 14:10–12; 1 Corinthians 3:11–15; 2 Corinthians 5:10; 1 Peter 4:5
Your words.	Psalm 19:14; Malachi 3:16; Matthew 12:36–37
Your thoughts.	Proverbs 15:26; 19:14; 94:11; 139:2, 23; Isaiah 55:7; Matthew 9:4; 15:19; Romans 2:15–16; Hebrews 4:12
Your secrets.	Ecclesiastes 12:14; Romans 2:16
Your motives.	Proverbs 16:2; 1 Corinthians 4:5
Your tears.	Psalm 56:8
Your prayers.	Revelation 5:8; 8:3–4
Your gifts to God.	Philippians 4:17–18; Hebrews 13:16
Your helping others.	Matthew 25:34–40
Your visiting those who need you.	Matthew 25:34–40

The above is obviously only a sample listing.
Heaven's record is much more extensive than you have
ever dreamed. If you have been living for God, seeking

every opportunity to show love to others, to love God, to be a blessing, to pray for others—if you have had streams of refreshment pouring out from your life to others (John 7:38), you probably remember only a fraction of the things for which God will one day reward you.

Occasionally God surprises us by letting us find out how He used some word we spoke or some action that we took years ago and perhaps forgot all about. About a century ago Stephen Grellat was led one day to go out to a heavily forested area of America to preach. It was a strong inward compulsion of the Holy Spirit. When he arrived at the loggers' camp, he found they had moved to another location, and their shanties were deserted. However, he was so sure he was sent by God that he went into an empty shanty and preached to the bare walls the sermon God had placed upon his heart. He then returned to his home. He could never understand why God would send him to preach to an empty shanty.

Many years later in England, as he walked across London bridge, a man grasped his arm. "I found you at last," the man said. "I think you are mistaken," said Mr. Grellat. "No. Didn't you preach in an empty shanty in the woods of America years ago?" "Yes," Mr. Grellat admitted, "but no one was there."

"I was the foreman in charge of the loggers," the stranger explained. "We had moved to a new location before I realized I'd left one of my tools behind. I returned to get it and heard a voice in one of the shanties; I peered through a crack between the logs and saw you. You never saw me, but I listened to the rest of your sermon. God touched my heart, and I became so convicted of my sin that after some time I purchased a Bible, repented of my sins, and became a Christian. Then I began to win my men to Christ. Your sermon has led at least a thousand people to Christ, and three of them have already become missionaries!"

That is the kind of surprise that heaven will reveal again and again.

In 1987, upon my return from ministry in Brazil, I stopped in Orlando, Florida, to attend a conference of mission executives. As I stood in the aisle before the first session, a mission leader whom I had never met suddenly threw his arms around me.

"Brother," he exclaimed, "I believe I am here because of you."

"Why, who are you?" I asked.

"I read in your book *Touch the World Through Prayer* of the night during World War II when God gave you a tremendous prayer burden as you asked God to stop the German pocket battleship disguised as a passenger vessel, the *Graf Spee*. [It had been sinking passenger ships with the loss of hundreds and hundreds of lives.] You told in your book how that very night the ship dashed into the harbor of Montevideo.

"My father-in-law was a British physician in South America. When World War II broke out, he took his family back to Britain to what he thought would be a safer place. His daughter was in love with an Argentine young man. After some months she decided to go back to him and get married. That very night my mother was on a British passenger ship just outside the harbor of Montevideo. If you had not prayed, the *Graf Spee* would have attacked that passenger ship, my mother would have gone down and been drowned. She would never have married, and I would never have been born. I am alive and in God's service today because of you."

Instantly I replied, "But there may have been a thousand other people praying at the same time."

"I don't know about the thousand," he said, "but I

know God put that burden on you and you prayed. I am serving God today because of you."

The man was Dr. Luis Bush, who, a few weeks later, became the leader of COMIBAM, the first All-Latin American Congress on World Evangelization, which was held in São Paulo, Brazil. He is the executive director of Partners International, the great missionary society. I still feel shocked to think how God used me, but only He gets the glory. Don't you suppose that is the kind of surprise heaven will contain for us, as again and again we are astonished to find how God has used our prayers, our finances, and our obedience to extend His kingdom?

Do you realize how important it is for you to be alert to bless others? to live for God? What activities that you engaged in today will add to your reward in heaven? Invest something each day for your reward. Are you measuring your life by the things God is measuring?

HOW HAS GOD BEEN MEASURING YOUR LIFE?

How does God measure life? How has He been measuring yours? Obviously, God does not measure life merely by chronology. "Do not forget this one thing, dear friends: With the Lord a day is like a thousand years, and a thousand years are like a day" (2 Peter 3:8). Life is more than days, weeks, and years. God's perspective on life is very different from our human perspectives.

The greatest life is not necessarily the life that is longest, busiest, or most famous. Lives of some of earth's great heroes are trivial in the measure of God and eternity. Probably most of the great ones, as evaluated by eternity, are overlooked in human history.

God's "do not forget" of 2 Peter 3:8 should alert us to our great danger. We are surrounded by such a totally secular culture that before we realize it we are evaluating people, activities, and life itself by the standards of that world. We need God's perspective on life and Christian living.

One day lived for God can equal the collected value of a thousand years. Time is significant with God if it is invested for Him. But wasted time is eternal loss. A thousand years of wasted time are not even worth a day in God's sight. John Wesley told his preachers, "Never be unemployed. Never be triflingly employed."

Does God measure life by the number of things you crowd into it? That depends on what you crowd into your life. Perhaps much of your life is already wasted—an eternal loss. Yet some of your choices and activities have had tremendous value in God's sight. Do you see how important it is to measure your life according to God's standards?

Beware of being today's hero, but tomorrow's fool! Beware of being great in the eyes of your family, your community, or your church. It is possible, even as a saved person, to be an eternal fool in the sight of God. What you do with your life after you are saved has tremendous eternal consequence (1 Cor. 3:11–15).

The Only Life Worth Living

The only life worth living is the life
    that's lived for God.
All else is but life thrown away and
    lacks the Lord's applaud.
The only life not lost is that you spend
    your God to please,
And values that you there would gain
    you here and now must seize.

The moments quickly fly away and then
    your chance is past;
The opportunity you see will not
    forever last.
The only time you have is now;
    the only day "today,"
And never does the past return;
    you go but once life's way.

All that you spend for earthly life
    you leave behind at death;
You say to it a last good-bye
    when comes your final breath.
All that you here for God invest
    you keep eternally,
You find it all and reap again
    when there your Lord you see.

Then what a folly to invest your all
    for fleeting time.
Not one such thing you find again on
    heaven's shore sublime;
But, oh, how wise to give your all—
    your time, your prayer, your love—
Investing for eternity and God's
    rewards above.

Wesley Duewel

3

IN HEAVEN, BUT . . .

Millions of Christians are going to discover that they are in heaven for all eternity, safe with God forever and ever, but that they lost a large part of their life's opportunities. They will receive praise from God, for everyone will receive some praise from God (1 Cor. 4:5). But they will discover with shock how much of life was wasted.

The most amazing experience of all eternity for many Christians, as well as unsaved people, will be at the time they stand before Christ's judgment throne. Every Christian will be there. God will confront all Christians with the way they spent their lives. It will be a day of great joy. But it will also be a day of great surprise.

A Christian lay dying. Suddenly he began to call out, "Lost! Lost! Lost!" A loved one, deeply shocked at his cry, hurried to his side. She thought that perhaps in his weakened physical condition he had lost his assurance of salvation and that Satan was accusing him. "Oh, no," he replied, "but I have wasted so much of my time and my life. I am saved by the grace of God, but I have lost the

27

rewards I could have had if only I had lived more out and out for God!"

Scripture teaches that we can build our lives on the foundation of Jesus Christ with either precious permanent spiritual materials or comparatively valueless materials that do not last (1 Cor. 3:11–15). This passage of Scripture is also written for Christians, who are to take it seriously. Paul says the day of judgment for Christians will evaluate what you and I did with our lives following our conversion.

The apostle explains that you can build your life on Jesus Christ (v. 4) (that is, you can be a true Christian) and yet do much of your building with wood, hay, or straw, instead of with gold, silver, or costly stones. How much of what you did today will be straw in eternity, instead of gold? Paul says anything you put into your life that is straw will be an eternal loss. It will be burned up.

Some things in your life and mine consume our time but have no lasting value. They do not increase physical health, mental health, or wisdom. Nor do they benefit our physical or financial needs. They do not help or bless others. They do not make you more competent in your skills. They are not necessary or helpfully productive.

Girolamo Savonarola (1452–1498), the Italian reformer and revivalist so mightily used by God before the time of the Reformation and who died a martyr when he was burned at the stake, preached, "Would you rise in the world? You must work while others amuse themselves. Are you desirous of a reputation for courage? You must risk your life. Would you be strong morally and physically? You must resist temptation. All this is paying you in advance. Observe the other side of the picture; the bad things are paid afterward."

All forgiven sins are judged at the Cross, and we will never meet them again (Heb. 8:12). It is not a question of sin. For Christians, the judgment throne of Christ is for evaluating their lives that they may receive their reward.

We must ask ourselves again and again whether this activity, this use of time or funds will be the "gold, silver, and costly stones" of 1 Corinthians 3:12. Or will it be "wood, hay, or straw" in God's sight at His judgment? Will this be something that God's judging fire will burn up, and throughout eternity I will have nothing to show for my Christian discipleship? Or will this be a loving, holy Christ who is pleased with my eternal investment whose benefits I will reap forever and ever?

In other words, are the things I am doing a wise and profitable investment of myself, my time, my talents, my funds? Or are they an eternal loss to someone in Christ's kingdom whom I could have blessed had I chosen to do so? When I stand before Christ's throne, will my investment be reported to my credit or to my shame?

Will the life I've lived be praised by Jesus for ministering to Him (Matt. 25:35–39)? When I ask in surprise on what occasion I ministered to Him, will He point to that which I have long forgotten, and say, "When you denied yourself and spent that time in prayer, or that time in blessing others, you were really blessing Me"? Or perhaps Christ will say, "That fifteen minutes, that hour you spent watching trivial TV, if only you had invested it in prayer, another person would have found the way to heaven. That money you spent on yourself needlessly could have extended my kingdom. You disappointed Me. You failed Me and others. You are saved forever, but so many aspects of your life are an eternal loss. You will not receive all the reward I so much wanted you to have."

LIFE IS A STEWARDSHIP

"You are not your own; you were bought at a price. Therefore honor God with your body" (1 Cor. 6:19–20).

Our bodies are not our own. They belong to Jesus. We have no right to squander our bodies with harmful habits or excess eating (the sin of gluttony). We have no right to shorten our lives by our habits, lack of exercise, or carelessness. Our bodies and lives (that is, our time) were purchased by Jesus.

Jesus owns us because He created us, and He owns us because He paid for us with His blood on the cross. To waste our bodies, our minds, our abilities, or our time is to rob Jesus. Just as certainly as not giving to God our tithe is robbing God (Mal. 3:8–9), so certainly wasting time, energy, or abilities is robbing God of a part of our lives. We belong to God (Rom. 14:8). We are to exalt Christ in and with our bodies (Phil. 1:20).

LIVING UNTO THE LORD

Living unto the Lord means to live for the Lord. Paul said, "To me to live is Christ" (Phil. 1:21). Certainly it means to live in holiness of life, in loving, living communion with Christ, in the consciousness of the Spirit's presence, seeking to please the Lord in all we do. It means acknowledging the lordship of Jesus over every aspect of our living. Every Christian, regardless of age, occupation, or sex is to live for the Lord.

Living for the Lord or unto the Lord does not put us into legalistic bondage. It does not conflict with employment responsibilities, home duties, or time for home relationships. It does not conflict with time for appropriate healthful relaxation, or for appropriate graciousness. One can be a good friend or neighbor as unto the Lord. Occasional social gatherings can be wholesome and refreshing.

But living for the Lord may shorten many a trivial conversation that merely "passes the time" or includes gossip or critical remarks. Such a lifestyle may, rather, invest time in prayer for others, blessing others, visiting the sick or elderly. It may change a "social butterfly" who flits from one social occasion to another to a person who volunteers time to help worthy organizations, to visit for the church, and purposefully to bear witness to Jesus' saving work.

Living unto the Lord will mean giving priority to personal Scripture reading, loving communion with Christ, and intercessory use of prayer lists, instead of spending hours watching TV programs that are neither educational nor uplifting spiritually, or otherwise wasting time in trivial pursuits. Living unto the Lord will introduce discipline into all aspects of life, into ways we spend money on ourselves, or on expensive time-consuming and nonproductive hobbies.

Most of us pass moments, minutes, and even hours in casual, frivolous matters that will make not the slightest difference in our welfare or lives. Twenty minutes redeemed from unimportant activity can be invested in prayer, in loving deeds in Jesus' name; and the twenty minutes invested may even result in your reaping benefits for twenty years to follow. More than that, they may bring you inestimable reward forever and forever in eternity. Twenty minutes may at times make a glorious difference in eternity. What fools we are to be careless with our time, our finances, and our abilities.

In other words, living unto the Lord means living for Jesus, living for the advance of His kingdom, living for eternity. It means living thoughtfully, prayerfully, and helpfully. It means seeking to bless as many as possible, seeking to save financially wherever possible in order to have more funds to advance Christ's kingdom and help others in need. It means to make our time, our talents, and our funds a trust from the Lord, to invest all under the

Spirit's guidance. In the words of John Wesley, "Earn all you can; save all you can; give all you can." It makes all of life a stewardship.

In order to help us invest ourselves for Christ and eternity, let us see the ways that God evaluates our lives. It will pay us eternally to measure our lives by the same standard God uses. We will thank Him over and over if we learn now to emphasize more fully the things that God is measuring.

Life Is Too Brief To Waste!

We march across the stage of time
    From dawn to set of sun;
We catch a glimpse of things sublime,
    Of work that must be done.
We plan for all that we would do
    And for our calling train.
We hope to see our vision through
    And real success attain.

How many finish earth's brief way
    Just when their work's begun,
And oft the noontide of life's day
    For them means setting sun.
How often in the prime of life
    Man puts his work aside,
And leaving children, home, and wife
    Confronts life's ebbing tide.

How many drop a cherished plan
    Just when success seems near,
When suddenly they find that man
    Is but a mortal here.
How many cherish long a goal
    That they would fain attain,
But that on which they set their soul
    How oft they fail to gain!

Life is too brief to lose one day
    E'en though your life prove long.
You pass but once along life's way,
    You sing but once life's song.
You have but one life to invest
    For ages without end.
You dare not fail to do your best—
    But one life do you spend.

God's daily guidance must be sought
   Or moments may be lost;
Your plans must all to Him be brought
   And you must count the cost.
God help you His own will to choose
   And His own work to haste.
You dare not life's brief moment lose—
   Life is too brief to waste!

                    Wesley Duewel

4

THE GOD WHO SEES AND MEASURES

Yes, God is a God who measures. This is evident repeatedly in His Word. He is a God who plans for the ages, and a God who notes the most minute details.

He is a God who counts. God "determines the number of the stars and calls them all by name" (Ps. 147:4). "The very hairs of your head are all numbered" (Matt. 10:30). God gave exact instructions to Moses about numbering the people of Israel, exact measurements to Moses for creating the tabernacle, and He records exact measurements for the New Jerusalem in the book of Revelation.

God could not be the creator of the universe if He were not a God exacting in His measurements. Astronomy is often considered a division of mathematics because of its constant dependence on and use of precise higher mathematics. Scientists have at times said God must be a mathematician! Of course, He is. He is a creator of mathematics. No human being can match the complexity and precision of God's mathematics. That is why we can set our clocks by the movement of the stars.

But He is much more than a mathematician. So it is

not surprising that in His omniscience God and His host of angels observe all people and are aware of everything that happens in the universe. They observe, understand, and record absolutely everything.

David writes, "O LORD, you have searched [a Hebrew word that means a careful investigative examination and searching, probing for details] me and you know me. You know when I sit and when I rise; you perceive my thoughts from afar. . . . You are familiar with all my ways. Before a word is on my tongue you know it completely, O LORD" (Ps. 139:1–4).

Yes, no one in heaven or on earth knows such a record of even one person like God does. Yet He has that record for every person who has ever lived. Such a chronicle is absolutely necessary if He is to be the Judge of all the earth (Gen. 18:25). No one but God is qualified to be our final Judge. He is the only one who knows all of the history of all our thoughts, desires, problems, experiences, choices, fears, hopes, and prayers. Before He can give just and right judgment of anyone, He must be perfect and total in His comprehensive knowledge.

For a sinner, this is a terrifying thought. God knows every sinful thought, desire, motive; He knows about all of our anger, lust, hatred, and actions. God knows the continuing influence on others of all one's sinful words and actions, one's sinful example. Only God has seen all, knows all, recorded all, and can comprehend all and fit the appropriate punishment that will be endured by the sinner for all eternity.

For the Christian, what a comfort, what a blessing, what a glorious hope is involved in having such an all-knowing, all-seeing, all-understanding, all-recording, and all-rewarding God! Our God is both Judge and Father. He is thrilled to see that we get all the reward that He can justly give to us. There has to be an adequate basis to His reward. Therefore, He eagerly takes into consideration every aspect of our lives that can possibly add to our reward.

A day or two after my wife and I arrived at the first missionary's home in North India where we were guests, a local citizen came to welcome us. On the missionary's wall was a Christian motto that said:

> God sees
> God hears
> God knows

When I first saw it, I questioned why such an obvious fact was put on a motto. I was soon to learn how revolutionary this truth is in India.

When this prominent person stepped into the room to greet us, he sat down and saw these words. In astonishment he exclaimed, "God sees! God hears! God knows! Why! How wonderful!" You see, he had never known of a God who could see, hear, and know everything.

Do you realize how wonderful it is that God knows every thought, desire, word, and deed? That is why God promises us, "Before they call, I will answer; while they are still speaking I will hear" (Isa. 65:24). It was true for Daniel. "While I was still speaking and praying . . . while I was still in prayer," God's angel came (Dan. 9:20–21). Gabriel came to Daniel with the answer before he had finished praying.

If there is one thing more wonderful than God's seeing and knowing your prayer, loving holy thoughts, and everything you ever do for Jesus' sake with your time, your strength, or your skills—if there is one thing more wonderful, it is that Jesus has a completely detailed record kept in heaven. He is planning to reward you for every loving desire and prayer, every loving deed you ever thought, spoke, or did! You, whoever you are, old or young, whether in your own home or out in public, can invest yourself for heaven's rewards. Are you aware of what is being recorded for you?

God's infinite knowledge, supplemented by His angels' information-gathering and recording system, keeps God constantly informed, constantly available, constantly ready to meet our needs. Furthermore, this wonderful massive record of all we think and do overlooks nothing that can add to our eternal reward.

God is constantly seeing, knowing, evaluating, measuring, and understanding. His angels are always busy keeping the record perfectly up to date. How does God constantly compile, evaluate, record, and keep this information available and up to the moment? Heaven doesn't need a computer system. God has a way infinitely above and beyond anything humans have ever conceived or invented!

Yes, God sees, measures, and knows all. His measurement of your life and mine is infinitely more complete and perfect than any human measurement or evaluation. It is constantly understood by God's loving heart. He is eagerly awaiting the day when He can confer on you your amazing reward.

We need to understand what God is measuring, what is important to Him, on what basis He is planning to give us such wonderful rewards. This is the purpose of this book. It describes eighteen aspects of your life that God is evaluating. Don't be ignorant or forgetful one day longer of what God is measuring in your life. Measure your life by God's standards! Don't lose your potential reward!

Lord, Make Us Saints of God

Lord, come upon Your Church today
 And make us saints of God, we pray.
Make us sufficient for this hour;
 Make us examples of Your pow'r.
Make us just what we ought to be
 So all Your presence in us see.

Lord, place Your hand on us again;
 Make us anointed, godly men.
Fill us and set our hearts aflame;
 Make us an honor to Your name.
Cleanse us and make us Spirit-filled
 So we can do all You have willed.

Lord, make us equal to the need,
 Anointed in each word and deed,
Each moment under Your command,
 Each moment guided by Your hand.
Prepare and use us hour by hour,
 Sealed by Your Spirit and Your pow'r.

Lord, make us saints of God indeed;
 Upon Your urgent errands speed.
We dare not carry on "somehow";
 Give us Your holy triumph now.
Each moment help us all invest
 For things eternal, true and best.

Wesley Duewel

5

MEASURE YOUR LIFE
BY LOVE

There is nothing in your life more important to God than your love. You are what you love. You are as great as your love, but no greater. Satan wants you to forget how important your love is in the sight of God. From the earliest days of the human race God has been trying to teach us to love.

The Jehovah-Elohim who came to the Garden of Eden to walk and talk with Adam and Eve was none other than the preincarnate Jesus, the eternal Immanuel, God with us. Why did He come to them? Because He loved them so. Because He wanted to develop their love and devotion. God is love, eternally He is love (1 John 4:8, 16).

What did God want from us above all else? Our love. Before Moses' death, when he reviewed for Israel the great things that God had told him, after reporting the Ten Commandments again, he told how the Lord said to him, "Oh, that their hearts would be inclined to fear me and keep my commands always!" (Deut. 5:29). Then Moses summed it up. He said, "Hear, O Israel: The LORD our God, the LORD is one. Love the LORD your God with

41

all your heart and with all your soul and with all your strength" (Deut. 6:4–5).

Over the centuries in their temple worship and in their synagogues, even in their homes twice each day— morning and evening—Jews have repeated verse four, but usually have omitted verse five, which goes with it. They also should have repeated twice each day the command to love God. They should have repeated it to their children, when they talked in their home, when they walked on the road, when they lay down at night, and when they arose in the morning (Deut. 6:5–9). They should have reminded themselves to love God with all their heart, soul, and strength.

Jesus emphasized this in the New Testament. When asked what was the most important commandment, He replied, quoting both verses four and five. It is not enough to believe in the unity of God. We must love Him supremely. And He added that the second commandment in importance is to love our neighbor as ourselves (Mark 12:29–31). This is the heart of Old Testament religion and the heart of New Testament religion. Love God supremely, and love others as yourself.

MEASURE YOUR LOVE FOR GOD

God measures our lives by our love for Him. Any life can be great in the sight of God, for anyone can love God greatly. Often the child loves as much or more than the adult. It is not a question of age, sex, wealth, education, or position. The humblest widow, the poorest layman, the most unnoticed Christian may love God as deeply as the most renowned church leader. God wants love to be your first priority, and He is grieved when you neglect your first love.

Enoch was great because His love for God was great.

David was a man after God's own heart (Acts 13:22) because he had a heart for God; he longed to be with God, in His presence, more than all else. Mary's greatness was the greatness of love, and John was greatly beloved because of his great love. Bernard of Clairvaux, mystic, theologian and hymn writer, said, "We know God only as far as we love Him." That person is greatest in God's kingdom of love who loves most—be he child or adult, man or woman, new convert or mature saint.

How can you measure your love for Him? By the practical things in your life.

1. *Measure your life and love by the number of times you lovingly think of Jesus during your day.* Don't try to keep a literal count. But punctuate your hours each day again and again and again by an "I love You, Jesus!" If you love Him enough, you will make it your habit whenever your mind is free for a few moments to breathe an additional "I love You, Jesus!"

When you walk to another room, sit down in your car to drive, stop at a traffic light, or pause for a moment—tell Jesus you love Him. If that seems unnatural to you, your love for Jesus is not yet so deep as it ought to be.

Among your first waking thoughts in the morning, among your last thoughts as you lie down at night, tell Jesus you love Him. When you bow your heart a silent moment before you eat, when you pick up your Bible to read a daily portion, when you walk into your church sanctuary, when you see a beautiful aspect of nature, when you pause to wash your hands or comb your hair, don't forget to tell Jesus again that you love Him. Find those free moments over and over each day. Look into His face and love Him.

2. *Measure your love by the degree of hunger you have to read His Word.* Measure it by the amount of time you save

to read His Word, by the joy with which you take His Word in your hand when you are alone with Him. The more you love Him, the more precious will His Word become to you. Measure your love by the activities you gladly do without in order to have more time with God's Word, the columns you omit reading in your newspaper or the programs you don't watch on TV in order to have more time to read His Word.

3. *Measure your love for Jesus by the number of things in your life that you adjust because you long to please Him.* How do you use your money? How do you economize so you can give more to advance Christ's kingdom? How do you rejoice in self-denial for Jesus' sake? How do you use your leisure time because you love Him? How do you adjust your priorities because of your love for Jesus?

4. *What are the little ways you try to bless others because of your love for Jesus?* How often do you say a "God bless you"? How often do you deliberately smile at others for Jesus' sake? How often do you try to keep a smile on your face as you sit in church, as you drive down the street, as you walk into a store, and you do it for Jesus' sake?

5. *What more can you do today to show your love to Jesus?* Make your love more real than it has ever been before, more practical, more joyous, more constant. Be a great lover of Jesus.

MEASURE YOUR LIFE BY LOVE FOR OTHER CHRISTIANS

God is measuring your love for your fellow Christians. Is it largely nominal, or is it living, burning in your heart? Is it practical? You cannot love God without loving His other children. God knows that if you don't really love the other believers you don't really love Him.

"Dear friends, let us love one another, for love

comes from God. Everyone who loves has been born of God and knows God. Whoever does not love does not know God, because God is love. . . . Since God so loved us, we also ought to love one another. . . . If we love one another, God lives in us and his love is made complete in us" (1 John 4:7–8, 11–12). "Anyone who does not love his brother, whom he has seen, cannot love God, whom he has not seen. And he has given us this command: Whoever loves God must also love his brother" (vv. 20–21).

If you love God, you quickly recognize the love of God in others. Love for fellow Christians tends to transcend all that separates us from them. It breaks down all barriers. It melts all hindrances. It shows in all activities and in all places. It transcends the false separations and antagonisms of race, nationality, caste, position, authority, education, and custom.

Love is realistic. It recognizes differences and values them. It overflows beyond them. Love for fellow believers opens your eyes and your heart. It dissolves prejudice, misunderstanding, and suspicion. Christian love heals hurts and even deep wounds. Love for one another draws Christians together and unites us. The more you love your fellow Christians, the more God pours His love into your heart. The more you take your fellow believers to your heart, the more God draws you to His heart.

Moses was great because of his great love for the people of God. They criticized and rejected him, but he still loved them. He was willing to pay a tremendous price in order to keep loving them and to keep faithful to them. Nehemiah, Daniel, and Hosea were all great because of their great love for the people of God. They identified with them, even weeping for them and taking their sins upon themselves in intercession.

The greatness in the sight of God of the one who loves his brother is shown by John in the verses we just read. He also shows the impossibility of having a great love for God unless it is accompanied by a great love for others. Paul's hymn of praise to love (1 Cor. 13) is this love of the brothers and sisters, and Paul's life exemplified the love he sang. Day and night he prayed for the believers. Constantly he lived for them. He was ready to pour out his life for them.

How can you measure your love for your fellow believers and for the church for which Jesus died?

1. *Measure your love by the joy you have in thinking of your brothers and sisters in Christ.* Do you think often of them and pray for them? Can you rejoice when they rejoice? Can you do this concerning all your fellow Christians? Is it really a joy to look forward to church services and to mingling with other believers?

2. *Measure your love by your willingness to overlook the failures, mistakes, weaknesses, and shortcomings of your brothers and sisters.* Measure your love by your ability to overlook and forgive when they forget you, slight you, or overlook you. Can you forgive them so fully that you can meet with them without feeling awkward or hesitant?

3. *Measure your love by your refusal to repeat rumors about fellow Christians unless there is genuine proof and a real need that this information be passed on.* Do you really feel grieved when one of them fails or sins? Can you still love them and pray for them then?

4. *Measure your love by your looking for ways to be a blessing to fellow believers.* Measure your love by your joy in doing extra little things to please or bless others, even, if possible, without their knowing whose kindness and love it was.

Undoubtedly that life is great in the sight of God that is filled with love. Love for God must have first place, but love for people is closely associated with it. Love for people does not guarantee love for God; but love for God brings love for people.

MEASURE YOUR LOVE FOR THE UNSAVED

God loves the unsaved so much that He gives His sunshine and rain, His blessings of health and long life to the saved and to the unsaved. He loves every sinner with the same infinite love with which He loves you. True, He cannot express the intensity and the intimacy of His love to those who do not respond to Him, but He loves them, longs for them, and delights to bless them just because He is love. To what extent is your love like that?

Is it far more difficult to love those who go on blatantly and heedlessly in their sin? It takes God's grace to love those who annoy us, pester us, and even harass us. Love triumphs over mistreatment, defilement, and persecution. Measure your love by its copying the love of Jesus. Measure your love by its perseverance. Measure your love by Calvary.

Love has a language that transcends all language, all barriers, all distances. Love has eyes to see hope, potential, and what the sinner can be by the grace of God. Love has eyes to see and understand. Love has ears to hear the heart in spite of the angry words of the speaker. Love has hands to give a transforming, miracle touch. Measure your life by your love!

1. *Measure your love by your hunger for the salvation of the unsaved.* Jesus often longed and wept for Jerusalem (Luke 13:34). Do you hunger and thirst for the unsaved of your family? your community? your nation? I have precious memories of a Christian young man who pleaded and wept night after night for a sinful large American city, its drunkards, its criminals, and its sin-slaved people. I

roomed across the hall from him, and every night I could hear him as he wept and prayed. What unsaved people do you hunger for so deeply that you weep?

Paul testified that he had great sorrow and unceasing anguish in his heart as he longed for the salvation of his people (Rom. 9:1–3). Do you know by experience what Paul was writing about? Without being heartbroken, can you see people around you living and dying in their sin? Measure your spiritual life by your love for the unsaved. Are you helping Jesus carry the burden for your world? Great will be the joy you bring to the heart of God if you do. Great will be your reward also.

2. *Measure your love for the unsaved by the extent to which you seek for their salvation.* The Father heart of God has a seeking love for every prodigal son or daughter. The Son of Man came to seek and save the lost. The Holy Spirit seeks on in persistent love for those sinning so rebelliously and hatefully. The only way the lost sheep can be found is for someone to seek for it. God's seeking love goes to all lengths to draw the sinner to Himself.

The more you as a Christian love God the more you love the lost. Your heart is possessed by the redemptive love of God. You long to love the unlovely, to bind up the wounds, to guide the straying, to lift up the fallen, to mend the broken, to help the helpless, to set free the enslaved, to encourage the discouraged, and to see the sinner saved and transformed by the love of God.

How far are you prepared to go to win a sinner to Christ? How low are you willing to stoop to lift a fallen one? How painful a price are you prepared to pay to prove Christ's love to a lost one? Measure your life by your seeking love for the lost. Is anyone's salvation important enough to you that for Jesus' sake you are really hungering and seeking for that person to come to a saving relationship?

How soon do you become weary in your seeking when all your attempts to show love are rebuffed and spurned? Often the people most resistant, most strong-willed are the people who can become the most all-out Christians once they are saved. Measure your spiritual love by your willingness to love on when all hope seems almost gone.

Love never gives up. Love never despairs of anyone. Charles Cowman, founder of OMS International, had that kind of love. He was great in love before he became great as a missionary statesman. As a successful business executive, he made Chicago's "Little Hell" his first mission field. He loved the desperate men on whom others had given up. He prayed into the night with drunkards, gamblers, and abandoned men who had tried again and again and failed. Cowman's love trusted when others no longer trusted. Converts from among the "down-and-outers" became some of his most ardent supporters in the early days of OMS. Nothing conquers like love. Love wins when all else fails. Measure your life by love!

3. *Measure your love for the unsaved by your intercession for them*. Jesus' love for the sinner was measured by His Gethsemane pleading for their salvation, by His prayer for their forgiveness on the cross. Is your love for the unsaved merely a theoretical love, or is it a Gethsemane love? Measure your spiritual love by Gethsemane love.

What testimony to your love for the lost does your prayer list give? How many unsaved are on your daily prayer list? How many on your list do you really hunger for, constantly intercede for? Do you ever fast for the salvation of someone on your prayer list? Is your love a truly interceding love? Measure your love by the intercession of your soul.

Do you carry a true prayer burden for the lost? Do

you sorrow at every evidence of the destructiveness of sin in the lives of others? Do you grieve at every indication of sin's further enslaving power? Do you sorrow for the sinner in his brokenness? Measure your love by the depth of your prayer burden for the lost.

Measure your spiritual life by your love—by your ardent, joyous, burning love for Jesus. Measure your life by your love for the church and for your individual brothers and sisters—not just two or three of your special friends, but for all of your brothers and sisters in Christ. Measure your spiritual life by your Christlike longing for the lost, by your undaunted seeking love, by your Gethsemane intercessory love for the lost. Measure the dimensions of your spiritual life by love.

God measures our lives by love. Though we have all knowledge and ability and have not love, we are nothing. Though we make all forms of sacrifice but have not real burning love for God and our sisters and brothers, we have nothing. Though we love many people, if there are those we do not love, our love is as nothing. How will your life measure in the light of Calvary, in the light of eternity? Will it be said of you: "See how greatly he loved" (John 11:36)?

The Greatest of These Is Love

Great is the faith that can mountains move;
    Great is the hope that is e'er renewed.
Great all the fruits of the Spirit prove—
    But the greatest of these is love.

God longs for loyalty in His own;
    God longs for faith placed in Him alone.
God longs for service to make Him known;
    But He longs above all for love.

God marks the doctrines that we profess;
    God notes the standards that we confess.
God sees our conduct in holiness—
    And He notes above all our love.

Spirit of God, on Your people fall;
    Come in Your fullness on great and small.
Come, live in fruitfulness in us all,
    But more than all else give love,

Wesley Duewel

6

MEASURE YOUR LIFE
BY COMMUNION

How does God measure your life? In the last chapter we meditated on how God measures our lives by our love. But there are other measurements. Let us consider your life as you express your love to Christ in communion.

No one's life is greater than his prayer. No one's influence is wider than his prayer. No one's spiritual power is greater than his prayer. Prayer has two main phases—communion and intercession. Both are measured by God. The greatest lives in eternity will not be measured by the number of years lived or by position or fame. Those lives are preeminently the greatest that have the greatest preciousness to God because of holy communion in prayer and because of prevailing holy intercession for others.

Measure your life by your communion with God. That life is greatest in the sight of God that means most to God. God values that life most that knows the closest fellowship with Him. Your importance to God is not measured by how influential the position is that you hold nor by the amount of human praise which you receive.

No doubt there are hidden saints on beds of pain whose friendship means more to God than that of many famous pulpit orators who seem to sway thousands. Anyone who is willing to draw near to God can be a close friend of God.

But who takes time to spend in communion with God? Who really believes that it is more important to take time for loving fellowship with God than to work an extra hour to make their work for God more perfect? Who really believes that it is important to take time to love Jesus? We do take time to show our love to our family. We take time to show friendship to our friends. Then why do we seldom go to God except when we want something from Him? Why is so much of our prayer asking? Why do we neglect to show daily personal love to Jesus?

The more we love God, the more we will delight to be with Him. The more we love Him, the more eagerly we will seek ways to get more time to be alone with Him. If there is one human being with whom we would rather spend our time, God does not have first place in our life. If there is one human being with whom we more eagerly share our joys, our thoughts, our plans, and our activities, then that person means more to us than God does.

God brought you into the relationship of sonship—not to give you more prestige, but that you might have the closest of fellowship with Him. Christ has chosen you to be part of His bride, and He showers His love and goodness on you—not to get you to work harder for him, but that He might draw you to Himself in the closest possible love relationship. More than He desires your time in service, He desires your time in communion. More than He desires your sacrifice, He desires your loving thoughts and words. Jesus appreciated the faithful, loving service of Martha. But it was Mary who drew closer to Him (Luke 10:38–42).

The primary purpose of Christian worship is not to be informed about God, but to have fellowship with God. The primary purpose of the only repeated New Testament sacrament is that you continually draw near to Him in the closest of spiritual communion at the Lord's Table. The primary purpose of His daily visit to your home is not to hear your complaints, nor even to hear your requests. He knows what you need before you ask Him. "Delight yourself in the LORD and he will give you the desires of your heart" (Ps. 37:4). The primary purpose of His daily presence with you is that you sit at His feet, that you make Him your closest Friend, your dearest Confidant, your heavenly Bridegroom.

A primary reason why God created human beings was for fellowship, for God is love. God's first relationship to Adam and Eve in the Garden was that of fellowship. God's relation to Enoch is only briefly mentioned in Scripture. But Enoch's fellowship with God must have been unusual communion. God had begun communion with Adam and Eve, but they did not respond wholeheartedly. They did not treasure it like they should have.

Enoch was the first person really to commune with God. All we are told is that Enoch walked with God for three hundred years. At last God had found communion and companionship. Think of it, three hundred years of heart-to-heart sharing. What did they talk about? What did God share with him? Surely in the sight of God Enoch was one of the greatest persons of history. God has kept the secret record of their fellowship as His own treasured possession.

When Christ became incarnate, He sought homes where He found fellowship. He took with Him Peter,

James, and John because of their closer fellowship. He preferred Mary's fellowship to Martha's service. Salvation is offered to us in order to restore us to God's fellowship. God takes us to His eternal home because He desires our eternal fellowship. Heaven is perfect fellowship.

How about your life? How important is your life to God? What holy satisfaction do you bring to God each day? Your service is important to God, but your communion is much more important. Service that flows from a communing heart has tremendous power and is tremendously effective in the sight of God.

It seems that God can find a thousand people eager to serve Him before He finds one whose great hunger is to commune with Him. Communion does not make you a recluse. Communion does not make you impractical or of little earthly use to others. It qualifies you to carry the presence of God with you and make all of your life a holy and fragrant blessing to others.

You don't lose time spent in communing with God! You invest it in the very heart of God. You invest it with the supreme Being of the universe. You can become one of earth's privileged few if you really commune with God. You can become one of the princes or princesses of eternity if now you will truly give yourself in daily communion with God.

A communing heart almost unconsciously becomes an interceding heart. Why? Because your communion is with Jesus and He is the great High Priest/Intercessor. As you commune with Jesus, He shares with you His holy heartbeat, His hunger for a whole world.

When you start your prayer time with intercession, it sometimes takes a while before you are supremely conscious that you are in the Holy of Holies with God. But when you begin your time with God with unhurried, priceless communion, you find yourself in heaven's throne room. You find yourself joining the seraphim and angel hosts in worshiping, praising, and adoring the Father, Son, and Holy Spirit.

When you are communing, really communing, you live on holy ground. You often find yourself in God's all-glorious presence. You become a truly beloved one to God. You may even sense the King extending His golden scepter, as it were, and saying, "Ask what you will, my beloved."

In the spiritually dark years before the Reformation, a hungry-hearted French Catholic lady, Madame Guyon, learned to walk in love and faith with Jesus. In the midst of great persecution, during which she spent ten years in prison and another seven years in banishment, God taught her mighty spiritual truths as she communed with Him. She wrote about the things of the spirit that she learned, and her writings are still popular today.

She lived a life of such sweet communion. Jesus was the Beloved of her soul. "His operations were so powerful, so sweet, and so sacred all together that I could not express them. Oh, what unutterable communications did I experience." "The stones of my prison looked in my eyes like rubies."

Although she wrote voluminously—sweet poems and hymns of love to Jesus, sixty volumes of books including one commentary—yet she lived a life of almost constant communing prayer, praise, and love to Jesus. She led many into salvation by faith and into the glory of a Spirit-filled life. Wherever she visited, revival came. She, "all ablaze with the unction and power of the Holy Spirit," spoke of her life of communion as "all holy, heavenly, inexpressible."

Miss Aletta Jacobsz, South African YWCA counselor, came to Korea in the autumn of 1938 because one of her converts, Miss Eunice Marais, was a new missionary under OMS International. Miss Jacobsz was a quiet Dutch Reformed lady with a life of amazing communion with Jesus. He was the most real person in her life. She spoke to whomever she met of Jesus and her love for Him.

Her spare moments were spent communing with her beloved Lord. Soon word spread among the missionaries, not only of OMS but of all denominations, of her beautiful walk with Jesus. The missionaries were in the vacation hill station of Whajinpo. She was asked to lead one of the daily prayer meetings for the deepening of spiritual life.

Her rapturous love for Jesus attracted to her door missionary after missionary of all denominations for conversation and prayer. She was asked to conduct a week's meetings. Wherever she went revivals broke out. Presbyterians, Methodists, and others as well as OMS people invited her to their mission stations. At least 110 missionaries' lives were transformed. Those I have known were permanently blessed, transformed, and filled with the Spirit.

The basis of it all was a life of amazing communion with Jesus. She was not primarily a speaker or Bible teacher—yet in only a few months she was used of God to bring new spiritual freshness and power to hundreds. Her communing love and radiant joy in Jesus set people ablaze for God. Her death at sea at the age of thirty-three during World War II brought her face to face eternally with her Beloved.

Oh, measure your life by the time you spend in the Holy of Holies. You will not want to speak of it much to others. It is your sacred trysting time—with Jesus, most of all, but also with the Father and the Spirit. If you speak too much about it, you might lose it. But pursue your holy Beloved until you find Him in all His beauty and glory.

Measure your life by the closeness of your communion with Christ. You can become great in the sight of God by living closely to the heart of God. That is why God was so pleased with Abraham His friend, David the shepherd boy, Mary the loving hearted, and John the beloved. You can bring more joy to the heart of God in communion than in any other way. Measure your life by the closeness, the joyousness, the preciousness of your communion and fellowship with God.

Sing this beautiful hymn with me. It was written by an Indian sister who lived just a half mile down the road from where we later spent twenty-five years of missionary service in Allahabad, India. Sing it with me:

> In the secret of His presence
>   how my soul delights to hide!
> Oh, how precious are the lessons
>   that I learned at Jesus' side!
> Earthly cares can never vex me,
>   neither trials lay me low;
> For when Satan comes to tempt me,
>   to the secret place I go.
>
> When my soul is faint and thirsty,
>   'neath the shadow of His wing
> There is cool and pleasant shelter,
>   and a fresh and crystal spring;
> And my Saviour rests beside me,
>   as we hold communion sweet;
> If I tried, I could not utter
>   what He says when thus we meet.
>
> Only this I know: I tell Him
>   all my doubts and griefs and fears;
> Oh, how patiently He listens!
>   and my drooping soul He cheers:
> Do you think He ne'er reproves me?
>   What a false friend He would be,
> If He never, never told me of the sins
>   that He must see!

Would you like to know the sweetness
    of the secret of the Lord?
Go and hide beneath His shadow;
    this shall then be your reward;
And whene'er you leave the silence
    of that happy meeting-place,
You will surely bear the image of
    the Master in your face.

                          E. L. Goreh

Let Me Sit at Your Feet Today

Loving Lord, I am hungry to sit at Your feet
    Just to share Your communion so precious and sweet.
Oh,'tis bliss; oh, 'tis heaven with You thus to meet—
    Let me sit at Your feet today.

Loving Lord, let me listen to Your tender word—
    Sweeter voice neither angel nor man ever heard.
Let me listen till my heart is melted and stirred—
    Let me sit at Your feet today.

Precious Lord, let me listen for hours to Your voice;
    How it thrills all my soul! how it makes me rejoice!
Above everything else, this is my highest choice—
    Let me sit at Your feet today.

Let me drink in Your love as I gaze on Your face;
    Let me see all Your loveliness, beauty, and grace.
Let me linger beholding You; give me this place—
    Let me sit at Your feet today.

Wesley Duewel

7

MEASURE YOUR LIFE
BY YOUR INTERCESSION

Did you realize that one major way God measures
your life is by your intercession? Your earnest
prayer can expand your life beyond any other limits that
you can reach. Measure your life by your fervent,
prevailing prayer for others and for Christ's kingdom. At
testimony time in heaven when people thank you for your
prayers, how many will rise to thank God for your
prevailing intercession, for the holy influence of your life?
Measure the breadth, depth, height, and length of your
life by your intercession.

MEASURE THE BREADTH OF YOUR LIFE
BY YOUR INTERCESSION

Measure the breadth of your life. You can do it by
measuring your intercession. Measure your spiritual
stature by your prevailing prayer. Is your intercession
wide enough to include your whole community? How
regularly do you pray for your local officials by name? Do
you pray for the churches of your community? For their
pastors? Do your prayers include the schools in your

community? Do you carry a prayer burden for the youth of your area?

Have you been a spiritual watchman for your church? For your city? God's watchmen are responsible to see and pray. "I have posted watchmen on your walls, O Jerusalem; they will never be silent day or night. You who call on the LORD, give yourselves no rest, and give him no rest till he establishes Jerusalem and makes her the praise of the earth" (Isa. 62:6–7). This is God's call to you and me. We are to be watchmen for our churches, our cities, and our nation. We are to keep spiritually awake, and we are to pray.

Is your intercession wide enough to include your state? Do you pray for your governor, your senators and congressmen? Do you pray about the laws in your state? Is your intercession wide enough to include your nation? You are urged by Paul to pray for your nation. "I urge, then, first of all, that requests, prayers, intercession and thanksgiving be made for everyone—for kings and all those in authority" (1 Tim. 2:1–2). They need your prayer. God has been measuring your obedience to that command. Don't criticize your government if you are not truly praying for it. In other words, measure your life by your prayer list and your prayer time.

Do you pray by name for the other nations of the world? For world leaders? For world problems?

On one occasion at a social function in India where about sixty of us met with Prime Minister Nehru, we were suddenly told that he wanted to shake hands with us. We formed a line, and as the Prime Minister neared, I wondered what God would have me say in the brief moment I would have with him. I looked in his face and said, "Prime Minister Nehru, I pray for you each day!" He instantly looked me in the eye and said with feeling, "Thank you."

Measure the breadth of your life by the breadth of your intercession. Be a world Christian.

MEASURE THE DEPTH OF YOUR LIFE BY YOUR INTERCESSION

Most people live superficially. They are glad for their family, but they take no serious spiritual responsibility for their family. They do not really invest prayer in their family. And they are superficial about their church life. They are content to attend church and make at least a nominal contribution. They have never learned to carry a spiritual burden for the life and witness of the church and for its people. They scarcely do more than mention the church in their prayer. They have never wept in prayer for it, and they have never cared enough to fast and pray for it. How deep is your intercession for your church?

How deep is your intercession for anyone or anything? Do you know by experience what a prayer burden is? Do you love anyone or anything enough to carry a continuing prayer burden? Measure the depth of your life by the quality of your intercession.

Do you love enough to have a weeping heart as you intercede? Tears of self-pity are cheap. They are often carnal. But tears of love as you carry a prayer burden for others are precious and powerful in the sight of God. Such tears are biblical.

David felt a great spiritual responsibility for his nation. Enemies surrounded them and wanted to wipe them out. Of his prayer for his people, he said, "My tears have been my food day and night. . . . I pour out my soul" (Ps. 42:3–4). He knew God measured his prayer tears. "List my tears on your scroll—are they not in your record?" (Ps. 56:8). The psalmist wrote, "Streams of tears flow from my eyes, for your law is not obeyed"

(Ps. 119:136). Do you carry that kind of prayer burden for your people?

Israel survived and Jesus could be born in a Jewish home in fulfillment of Scripture because David, Isaiah, Ezra, Nehemiah, Jeremiah, and others known to God prevailed in intercessory prayer for the nation. In what ways will the kingdom of God advance because of your intercession?

Paul wept as he carried a tremendous burden for both Israel and the church. Jesus wept repeatedly as He prayed (Heb. 5:7). Are you Christlike enough to pray at times with tears for the lost, for your nation? Covet from God a weeping heart of longing intercession. Measure the depth of your life by the depth of your intercession.

MEASURE THE HEIGHT OF YOUR LIFE
BY YOUR PRAYERS

Measure the height of your life by the frequency with which your intercession really touches heaven. Cornelius was a Gentile, but he was faithful in his prayer habit. His prayer reached all the way to Christ's throne. Would you want God to measure your life by the extent and quality of your regular prayer times? He does. God sent an angel to assure Cornelius that his prayers had been reaching heaven (Acts 10:4, 30–31).

Daniel's prayers touched heaven. Three times God sent the angel Gabriel to assure him of that (Dan. 8:15–18; 9:20–23; 10:10–14, 18–19). How precious are these times when the Holy Spirit assures you that your prayers have touched the throne of God! Do the angels know you as one who often enters the throne room of heaven through your intercession? Are you well known among the angels? Measure your life by the height of your intercession.

John the beloved apostle was in the Spirit on the

Lord's Day (Rev. 1:10). The government of Rome had exiled him to the little rocky island of Patmos. He could no longer pastor his church in Ephesus, but he could intercede. It was probably at the church worship time that John was praying in the Spirit, and he was probably praying for his beloved Ephesian brothers and sisters of whom he was the pastor. John truly touched heaven and was in the heavenlies while he had his vision recorded in the book of Revelation.

Measure your life by heaven's touch upon you while you pray. Do you experience the glories of God's presence as you pray? Measure your communion by your joy inexpressible and glorious as you commune alone with Jesus. Measure your life by the height of your communion as you look into His face, and the height of your intercession as you sit with Jesus on His throne of intercession and intercede with Him for His kingdom (Rom. 8:34; Eph. 2:6).

MEASURE THE LENGTH OF YOUR LIFE BY YOUR INTERCESSION

The prayers of those who prevail in intercession live on and on. We are still reaping results from the prayers of David, Isaiah, Paul, and Jesus. We are still reaping fruit of the prayers of Luther, Wesley, Charles Finney, and E. M. Bounds. Prayers prayed in the Spirit often have multiple answers, repeated fulfillments. The answers to some prayers are like the river of Ezekiel 47. They flow wider and deeper over the years. They keep finding answers in lives of Christ's prayer warriors who augment these older prayers with their own. By the time we stand before Christ's judgment throne, a mighty stream of holy influence will flow over the earth. Those prevailing intercessions have been answered, reechoed, and reconfirmed again and again.

Are you prevailing in prayers that will live on and on? Any prayer prayed in the Spirit for the advance of Christ's kingdom, for God's blessing and revival in His church, for earth's harvest, for more reapers in God's harvest field, for a lost and tragically needy world—any such prayer is caught up with the intercessions of Christ on His heavenly throne (Rev. 5:7). The Holy Spirit has deepened your heart cry as you prayed. Christ is the heavenly Amen to your prayer (Rev. 3:14). That prayer can never die. It will live on in widening fulfillment until eternity.

How many mighty prevailing prayers of yours will be included in God's great volume of heaven-preserved prayers of the saints? No Spirit-motivated and Spirit-guided intercession that is still unanswered can ever be lost. Jesus has said His almighty Amen (Rev. 3:14). The incense of His prevailing in heaven will be added to your prayers and will have mighty fulfillment yet on earth (Rev. 8:1–5) and will hasten in the kingdom of Christ. Praise God!

Korean Christians of all denominations have a practice of attending daily early morning prayer meetings in their churches, which are held at 4:30 or 5:00. About one-third of our 600,000 believers in the Korea Evangelical Holiness Church (founded by OMS International) are in attendance each morning. But remember that for security reasons one adult must always stay in the home. The major portion of their prayer meeting time is given to actual intercession.

Measure the length of your life by your intercessions preserved in heaven, which will yet receive God's full and glorious answers. Any Christian, every Christian, can add breadth and depth and height and length to his life by joining in Christ's holy intercession, by being Christ's prayer partner, by being anointed by the Spirit to pray (Rom. 8:26), prevailing at God's throne as one of His faithful watchmen (Isa. 62:6–7).

You can do more to move the world for God on your knees than you can in any other way. You can bless more lives through intercession than you can in any other way. The greatest work that you will ever do for God is to intercede in accordance with His will. You can unite yourself more fully with the purpose and plan of God in prayer than you can by any other form of Christian service. You can more closely feel the pulse and loving heartbeat of the great heart of God in intercession than you can in any other way.

You lend a helping hand more quickly through prayer than in any other way. You lift heavier loads on your knees than in any other way. Your arms can embrace more of the world in Christian love through prayer than in any other way. You can wipe more tears from the eyes of the sorrowing, you can place a hand of blessing upon the heads of more children, you can lend a guiding hand to more youth, you can strengthen the hand of more Christian workers in prayer than in any other way—if you really intercede and prevail before God. Prayer does not take the place of any other helpful action you can do. But prayer must undergird all else you do. Prayer adds God's power to everything else you do. Not only so, but by prayer you can touch and help those you can bless in no other way.

But do you intercede? Do you know what it means to prevail in prayer on behalf of others? Do you often experience what Paul refers to as wrestling in prayer with forces of spiritual darkness (Eph. 6:12, according to the Greek; Col. 4:12)? Do you often pray with the self-denying intensity that Jesus indicated would characterize

His followers in these days when He said, "Then they will fast" (Matt. 9:15)? Is your prayer truly powerful and effective (James 5:16)?

Measure your life by your intercession. How much do you really know in your own experience of the secret of praying things into existence for God? Jesus said to His disciples, "Could you not keep watch with me for one hour?" (Matt. 26:40). Does He today still count the time you spend in prayer? If so, how often must you hang your head in shame because you fill your life with so many good things but omit that which Christ put first in His own life?

If you are to measure your life by your intercession, you must measure more carefully the time you are spending in prayer. Measure your life by the extent to which you know burden bearing in prayer. Measure your life by the number of times the Holy Spirit gives you a special prayer burden for an individual or a situation. Measure your life by the extent to which you pray till prayer becomes praise and you can claim victories by faith.

Measure your life by the number of the unsaved for whom you travail in prayer, by the number of Christian workers whose ministry you share through prayer, by the number of Christian training institutions, Christian literature agencies, Christian radio programs, and Christian organizations you uphold regularly in prayer. Measure your life by the length of your prayer list, by the extent to which you pray for all the countries of the world, nation by nation.

A Mrs. Knight, living in Palmerston North, New Zealand, caring for an ailing husband, told me she was on her knees each morning at 4:00 to pray for my ministry. A Mr. Wright in Upper Hutt, New Zealand, showed me his prayer room and his loose-leaf prayer notebook filled with maps, pictures of Christian workers, including mine, and told me how he spent much of his time each day, in his retirement now, interceding for God's work around the world. A retired Australian missionary couple in their eighties told me that for years they had been praying for my ministry and that they were on their knees at 4:00 each morning.

I know these people personally, but undoubtedly heaven's records list the prayer records of millions of God's saints whose prayer habits put us to shame. They are God's hidden prayer statesmen, the unknown heroes of Christ's kingdom. They will be honored before the whole world at Christ's judgment throne. You and I too should measure our life by our intercession.

Measure your life by your faithfulness in praying for Christians under persecution, Christians imprisoned or banished because of their faith, Christians leaving home and loved ones for the sake of witnessing and furthering the Gospel. Measure your life by your faithfulness in praying for rulers and all in authority in your own land (1 Tim. 2:1–2).

Measure your life by the extent to which you put other things aside in order to make time for prayer. Measure your life by your hunger to be alone with God in prayer. Measure your life by the extent to which all your life is filled with prayer and you pray without ceasing (1 Thess. 5:17). You are no greater, no more useful to God, and no mightier in the sight of God than your prayer. Heaven is measuring your life by your prayer. *What do you find the measure of your own life to be?*

Pray On

How often do you bear a burden
    In intercession for the lost?
How deeply do you feel compassion?
    Or do you shun to pay the cost?
Is prayer for you mere relaxation,
    A passing pleasure now and then?
Or do you pray in intercession
    With burdened heart for souls of men?

How often do you feel the hunger
    That cannot rest unsatisfied?
That keeps you praying ever longer
    Until the answer is supplied?
How often are you lost in praying
    Until, forgotten, pass the hours,
Until you wrestle, not delaying,
    And seize the vict'ry from hell's powers.

How often do the tears unbidden,
    Hot burning tears, course down your cheek
As on you pray and bear the burden
    And for God's promised answer seek?
'Tis then you go into the garden
    And share with Christ the sweat of blood;
'Tis then you lead lost souls to pardon
    And bring joy to the heart of God.

O saint of God, keep praying, pleading;
    Pray on, weep on, believe, and fast.
Faint not nor fear, keep interceding;
    God's hour of pow'r will come at last—
His perfect answer long awaited,
    Souls saved and Satan's full defeat,
Your long desire, with blessing freighted,
    And trophies to lay at His feet.

Wesley Duewel

8

MEASURE YOUR LIFE
BY JOY

T he second fruit of the Spirit is joy (Gal. 5:22). Can it be that next to your love, your joy is the most evident and most powerful witness to the Spirit's fullness in your life? The two priorities of the Holy Spirit in you are love and joy. Can it be that next to love, joy is the most powerful spiritual dynamic in your daily living? Love can impart spiritual power to your praying. Does joy also powerfully transform your praying?

New Testament Christianity is life-transforming joy. A holy person is a rejoicing person. Heaven is as full of joy as it is full of holiness and glory. Jesus Christ is the happiest being in heaven. He is distinguished above all others by God's anointing Him with the oil of joy (Ps. 45:7).

Happiness is fleeting; it tends to depend on circumstances. Joy can be permanent. It is part of your character. A habit of grumbling and complaining, a tendency to be negative, tells something about the level of your spiritual life. Measure the Spirit's work in your life by your deep abiding joy regardless of life's circumstances.

When God the Father sent Jesus to earth, He

anointed Jesus with the Spirit for multiple ministry. Not only was Jesus to preach good news to the poor, freedom for the captives, and release from darkness to light, He was also "to bestow on them a crown of beauty . . . the oil of gladness . . . and a garment of praise" (Isa. 61:3). Jesus was so blessed by His anointing with the oil of joy that He came to anoint us with joy. Spirit-filled Christians should be distinguished by God's anointing of joy. Measure your life by the joy of the Holy Spirit. Is the Spirit's seal of joy continually on you?

There are many forms of happiness and transient joy that may have little to do with spirituality. True spirituality is contagious with holy joy—the joy of the Lord. True spirituality is made strong by the joy of the Lord (Neh. 8:10). The joy of the Lord is an automatic way to let your light shine before others (Matt. 5:16). The Lord's joy in you promotes and strengthens the unity of God's people. It is a breath of heaven's air when a joy-filled, joy-radiating Christian enters a group.

Measure the joy of the Lord in your life. Is it normal for you to have a smile on your face? Is it spiritually normal for you to say encouraging words to people you meet? Is it known by others that you usually see the hopeful side of situations? Are you known for a strong spirit of faith when you face difficult problems? Are you known as a singing Christian? If you cannot carry a tune, are you nevertheless known for quoting choruses or joyful verses of hymns to others when they need such encouragement?

The Spirit-filled person is a realist. He is accustomed to fighting spiritual battles, but that does not rob him of his spiritual joy. The Spirit-filled person gladly helps bear the burdens of others. But as he does so, he shares a promise, quotes a verse of song, testifies to God's faithfulness, and often changes the whole atmosphere from fear or gloom to faith and hope.

The Christian life is not emotion. But the experience of salvation brings deeply satisfying emotions. No one can experience forgiveness, peace, assurance, victory over sin and temptation, and fellowship with God without experiencing great abiding joy. The measure of the mere nominalness or the deep reality of anyone's Christian experience can be known by the extent to which such terms are spiritually meaningful and satisfying. Many nominal Christians have never known what true spiritual joy is.

God created us to enjoy humor. Wholesome humor can often change the atmosphere from criticism, complaining, gloom, and dejection to normal wholesome living again. But much humor is superficial, cheap, and empty. Much laughter leaves you more empty than you were before. Too much humor today is vulgar and impure.

Don't get a reputation of being a clown, of always "goofing off," of never taking anything seriously. Don't take away God's presence from a sacred moment by an ill-timed or inappropriate joke. A London psychiatrist was visited by a man greatly depressed. The psychiatrist told him, "You ought to go and hear so-and-so (a renowned humorist and clown)." The man cried out, "I am that clown." Christian joy is not just humor.

There is an aesthetic joy in worshiping in a clean, beautiful church, with stirring music and well-loved hymns or choruses of worship. This may be wholesome joy, but spiritual joy is much deeper than this. There is a social joy in singing, praying, and fellowship with Christians of like faith. To hear Scripture read or to hear prayer by a dearly loved relative, pastor, or Christian in whom one has deep confidence may stir profound emotions but may be without true spiritual joy.

To read or hear the comforting words of Scripture in times of trial, suffering, or sorrow may bring confidence, assurance, and emotional satisfaction and joy. But this is not necessarily the joy of the Lord. In some groups where free forms of fellowship and worship are found, many may participate in saying "Amen," "Praise the Lord." Often this is merely the joy of loyal enthusiasm. None of the above-mentioned joys are in conflict with spiritual joy. They may even express spiritual joy. But they are all inadequate substitutes for it.

1. *Measure your fellowship with God by your joy in the Lord.* Measure it by your joy in private prayer. If you really love the Lord, it will be your great joy to be alone with Him. Time spent in private prayer can be so precious that often a half hour or hour will pass before you realize it. Christians who find it difficult or tiring to spend that much time in prayer prove that they know little of true spiritual fellowship and joy in Christ. Other people have undoubtedly been measuring your Christian experience by your spiritual joy. Does it manifest itself in your life? In your words? In your face? Heaven's joy beautifies the faces and lives of godly Christians on earth.

2. *Measure your spiritual fellowship by your singing to the Lord.* Every Christian enjoys singing about the Lord. Do you joy in singing *to* the Lord? Other people often measure the fellowship of two individuals by how happy they seem together.

Not every person can sing a solo or even carry a tune. But everyone can sing to the Lord. I had the joy of leading a Muslim college student to salvation. He had never read the Psalms. He had just begun to read the New Testament I gave him. But in his first audible prayer after his conversion, he prayed, "O Lord, You have put a song in my heart." I later found he could not carry a tune. But in his monotone he could sing to the Lord. And I am sure the Lord delighted to hear him.

When our son was about four years old, one day in the car he began to sing to the Lord. His song did not rhyme, it had no great musical quality, but he was singing from his heart as a child to the Lord he already loved. "Oh, Jesus, I love You so much. I'm glad You saved me and died for me," he sang. And I am sure Jesus heard him and smiled.

Followers of some religions chant the names of their gods or other monotonous repetitions, but Christ gives us a singing religion. Singing is not a part of public worship in other religions. But it is a natural part of Christian worship. Spiritual joy naturally expresses itself in singing.

3. *Measure your spiritual power by your joy*. The joy of the Lord imparts spiritual strength and is a measure of spiritual strength (Neh. 8:10). Spiritual power is the power of faith, and where there is faith there is joy. Doubt and discouragement weaken and are a measure of weakness. Spiritual power is the power of the Holy Spirit, and He is the Spirit of joy.

The kingdom of God is not measured by food and drink—by performance of religious duty, but by joy in the Holy Spirit (Rom. 14:17). Happiness is dependent upon circumstances. Abiding joy, in spite of circumstances, is the proof of a life strengthened by God. Christ gives this joy (John 17:13), His own joy, and we can measure His indwelling, His empowering, and the extent of His kingdom within us by our spiritual joy.

4. *Measure your fullness of the Spirit by your joy*. To be filled with the Holy Spirit is to be filled with joy also. Spiritual joy is "joy in the Holy Spirit" (Rom. 14:17). When you are filled with the Spirit, you rejoice and your heart sings to Christ (Eph. 5:18). The book that is said to

have led more people into the victorious Spirit-filled life than any other book, apart from the Bible, is *The Christian's Secret of a Happy Life* by Hannah Whitall Smith. To be full of the Spirit is to be full of joy. Measure your fullness of the Spirit by your joy.

Joy can be hidden deep in your heart where the eyes of others cannot see it. But it is natural for joy to express itself. You cannot succeed in totally hiding joy. People see it and heaven's angels see it.

Joy shows in the words you use and in the tone of your words. Joy expresses itself in your attitude toward others, in little deeds of love by which you rejoice to bless others. It shows in your countenance. When your soul is happy, your face testifies to it again and again.

Many a happy Spirit-filled Christian has been asked by others, "Why are you always so happy? As I have observed you, you don't seem to get gloomy and downhearted like others. What is your secret?" What an opportunity this gives to testify to your joy in the Lord! Measure your life by your spiritual joy.

There is joy in answered prayer, joy in fellowship with friends and fellow Christians, joy in sharing in worship, joy in service. But the greatest joy of all is joy in the person of Jesus. Measure your life by your joy in Jesus.

Many of God's children have testified that the secret of their spiritual lives was to get their souls full of joy each day in their times alone with God. They tried to do this before they met the general public. Then they could carry the blessing of the secret place out into their day's activities. I once knew a lady who was a cashier in her son's hardware store, who testified that before she met the public she prayed every morning until she felt God's presence and joy, and then she began her day's work. Measure your spiritual condition today by your joy in the

Lord today. You can know God's "inexpressible and glorious joy" (1 Peter 1:8). Measure your life by joy.

George Müller was taught by God that the most important daily spiritual priority was to be spiritually blessed to the point of joy in the Lord. "The first great and primary business to which I ought to attend every day was to have my soul happy in the Lord." A heart bubbling over with joy makes your life more attractive to the unsaved, is a powerful witness to Christ's grace, and makes a more lasting impact on others than almost any other aspect of your Christian life. Measure your own life's testimony by your joy.

The Christian's Joy

Oh, what joy to us is giv'n;
    Christ gives us the joy of heav'n!
He imparts true happiness;
    He who saves will daily bless.
Jesus Christ bestows a joy
    Naught on earth can e'er destroy.

There is nothing to compare
    With the joy true Christians share!
When the Holy Spirit fills,
    Heaven's joy inspires and thrills.
Miracles of grace surprise;
    Earth becomes a Paradise.

Joy brings strength and hope and peace;
    Joys from fear and doubt release.
Joy gives courage in the strife;
    Joy adds fragrance to your life.
Joy bestows a heavenly grace
    To your happy Christian face.

Oh! the joy to Christians giv'n!
    What a foretaste of God's heav'n!
What a joy unspeakable—
    More than tongue can ever tell!
When we know our Lord like this,
    Earth is heaven, life is bliss.

Wesley Duewel

9

MEASURE YOUR LIFE
BY YOUR FAITH

The essence of the Christian life is faith. We are saved by faith in Christ's atonement through God's amazing grace (Eph. 2:8). We are justified by faith and have access to God by faith (Rom. 5:1–2). We are purified by faith (Acts 15:9), sanctified by faith (Acts 26:18). We live by faith (Gal. 3:11). Christ dwells in our hearts by faith (Eph. 3:17). We approach God with freedom and confidence by faith (Eph. 3:12).

Through faith we inherit what God has promised (Heb. 6:12). Through faith we understand God's power, workings, and will (Heb. 11:3). Through faith, spiritual exploits for God are accomplished (Heb. 11:32–39). By faith we are victorious over opposition, suffering, and even death. From the moment of salvation to the entrance into heaven, faith is the all-important key to God. That is why at least twenty-one times the Bible refers to Christians as believers.

Jesus often measured His disciples' faith. Five times He said, "O you of little faith!" Three times He spoke of their lack of faith. He asked, "Do you still have no faith?" (Mark 4:40). "Where is your faith?" (Luke 8:25). Twice

He commended the faith of Gentiles who sought His help. He mentioned His disappointment at His disciples' little or no faith ten times. This seems to have been His greatest disappointment with them. Is Jesus satisfied with your faith?

Jesus urged the disciples to believe more. "Have faith in God" (Mark 11:22). His disciples asked for His help: "Increase our faith" (Luke 17:5). Christianity is called "the faith" (Acts 16:5).

Faith is one of the primary criteria by which God evaluates your spiritual life and your ministry. Faith is a key to much of the effectiveness of your prayer and your ministry. God constantly measures and evaluates it. The Bible speaks of little faith, no faith, dead faith, weak faith, deficient faith, useless faith, futile faith. It also speaks of firm faith, sincere faith, great faith, most holy faith, precious faith, growing faith, strengthened faith, increasing faith, and complete faith. Jesus is the author and perfecter of our faith (Heb. 12:2). People can be full of faith, just as they can be full of the Spirit.

God observes and measures faith so carefully because it is closely related to your walk with Him and to your effectiveness for Him both in prayer and in ministry. Faith produces obedience (Rom. 1:5). Faith protects as a shield (Eph. 6:16) and as a breastplate (1 Thess. 5:8). Faith is the victory that overcomes the world (1 John 5:4). Twice the Bible tells us to pursue faith (1 Tim. 6:11; 2 Tim. 2:22). Without faith it is impossible to please God (Heb. 11:6).

Faith is one of the most difficult aspects of your spiritual life to measure. (A) Faith is comparatively unseen except as it is evident in your prayer, your attitude, and your actions. (B) Faith may be accepted in heaven by God long before the answer is evident to you and others (Dan. 10:12–13). This, as in the case of Daniel, may be because the answer is delayed by Satan's spirit-warfare against

God's will. (C) Sometimes faith is more accurately measured by the calm inner assurance than by the outward evidences of God's answers. God's time is perfect time but not necessarily your time. Often He waits so that His answer may be greater, more gracious, and more miraculous for you and more glorifying to His name (Isa. 30:18).

1. *Measure your faith by the depth of your trust.* Trust is a deep confidence in God, in His love, wisdom, and power. Measure your life by the blessed assurance you have that God is in charge of your present and your future, your circumstances and all that touches your life. Measure your faith by the unwavering confidence that God is your Father and that He can work in all things for His glory and for your good (Rom. 8:28).

Measure your life by your undisturbed peace of heart in the midst of storm, your confident trust when you cannot see a path through your problems. Measure your faith by your ability to say with Job, "Though he slay me, yet will I hope in him" (Job 13:15). Measure your faith by your trusting assurance that your Father is too good to forget you, too wise to make a mistake, too loving to let you be ultimately hurt or be the loser, and too mighty to ever be defeated.

Measure your faith by your assurance that Jesus is with you. Among His last words before He ascended back to heaven were, "Surely I am with you always" (Matt. 28:20). When fear grips you, say, "Jesus is with me." When illness strikes, say, "Jesus is with me." When others misunderstand or oppose you, when you need to make a sudden decision, when financial need arises—whatever the circumstances, rejoice: Jesus is with you.

Dr. A. B. Simpson, while preaching in Ireland, asked, "What is it to abide in Jesus?" He gave his own answer, "It is to keep on saying minute by minute, 'For this I have Jesus!'" When he concluded his message, the pianist rose and said, "While you were speaking I was handed a telegram asking me to come home at once. My mother is dying. Instantly I said, 'For this I have Jesus,' and peace flooded my soul.'" With a radiant face, she continued to speak. "I have never traveled alone. For this, I have Jesus. I must take the midnight train tonight. For this, I have Jesus. I must catch the steamer and cross the sea. For this, I have Jesus. I must make a long journey to the south of England. For this and all else that goes with it, I have Jesus."

Later she testified that when she got home her sister fell on her neck, sobbing, "Oh, if you had come ten minutes sooner you would have seen mother." Instantly she said in her heart, "For this I have Jesus." The family was so upset that she had to take charge of funeral arrangements. Then she had the responsibility of working out legal details. But she kept saying to herself at every moment, "For this I have Jesus."

2. *Measure your faith by your obedience*. Trusting and obeying go hand in hand. Faith obeys just because God commands. Faith obeys and marches at God's direction to the bank of the Red Sea and lifts its foot to step into the water, and, lo and behold, God dries a path through the sea. Faith obeys even when it cannot see. Faith obeys even when the heart asks "Why?" Faith obeys even when those around misunderstand. Faith obeys even when the eyes fill with tears. Measure your faith by your simple trusting obedience to God.

3. *Measure your faith by your vision*. Measure your faith by your ability to see things from God's perspective. Measure your faith by your ability to take the long view. Faith obeys in the light of God's eternal plan. Faith is upheld by your vision of God's tomorrow. Measure your faith by your vision of God's faithfulness, by your

assurance that your vision is from God. Measure your faith by your vision of your future reward (Heb. 11:26). Measure your faith by your thrilling vision of God's greatness, God's goodness, God's nearness, God's unseen angels surrounding you (2 Kings 6:17). When God is for you, who can be against you (Rom. 8:31)? Measure your faith by your vision.

4. *Measure your faith by your outflowing streams.* "Whoever believes in me . . . streams of living water will flow from within him. By this he meant the Spirit, whom those who believed in him were later to receive" (John 7:38–39). Measure your faith by the outflow of the Spirit from your life. Measure your faith by the Spirit's outstreaming fullness. Measure your faith by rivers of blessing flowing from your life. Measure your faith by love replacing bitterness, joy replacing dreariness and despair, and life replacing death-like conditions wherever God sends you to bless others.

Measure your faith by your not being overcome by the circumstances around you, not being discouraged by the forces against you, and not being conformed to the world around you. Measure your faith by outflowing love, joy, peace, goodness, and every form of spiritual blessing. Measure your faith by the Spirit's artesian well pouring spiritual blessings out of your life day after day. The more you believe God, the more people will be blessed through you. The more you believe, the more the atmosphere around you will change. You take God into each situation that you enter by faith, and God's blessings then flow invisibly and at times even visibly from you to others in their need.

5. *Measure your faith by your initiative.* Measure your faith by your willingness to step out on the promises of God, by your ability, like Abraham, to start out obeying God even when you don't know where God is leading

you. Faith does not demand to see all the way ahead. It takes obedient initiative, willing to cross life's deserts with one day's manna at a time, willing to obey God today and leave tomorrow in His hand. Measure your faith by your eagerness and joy to launch out for God, by your willingness to start out into the deep of God's will, to give the shout of praise before Jericho's walls fall down. Measure your faith by your taking God's guided initiatives for His glory.

6. *Measure your faith by your ability to persevere.* Faith can labor on without growing weary in even the longest days. Faith can weather the most violent of storms. Faith can endure repeated setbacks. True faith can persevere.

Measure your faith by your ability to continue when others drop by the wayside. Measure your faith by your ability to push ahead when the waves are against you, when the night is dark around you. When all hope is gone, measure your ability to stand amidst your fearful friends and co-workers, like Paul, and say, "Keep up your courage . . . I have faith in God that it will be just as he told me" (Acts 27:20, 25).

Measure your faith by your ability to march around your Jericho seven days and on the seventh day to circle your Jericho seven times, though the world consider you a fool. Measure your faith by your ability to persevere like Moses in the face of massed opposition because you "see him who is invisible" (Heb. 11:27). Measure your faith by your ability, like Abraham, to disregard all the contradicting evidence of the natural, to look all the facts in the face (Rom. 4:18–21), and to believe in God's supernatural answer, to be fully persuaded that God is still able.

Adoniram Judson is famous for his oft-quoted statement, "The outlook is as bright as the promises of God." Again, he wrote, "If they ask, 'What prospect of ultimate success is there?' tell them, 'As much as there is an almighty and faithful God, who will perform His promises.' "

It was that faith that kept him and Ann, his first wife, laboring for seven years before they baptized their first convert, and after twelve years had only eighteen. It was faith that carried them on when their first baby died, faith that kept him plodding till he wrote a Burmese language grammar and dictionary and after ten years completed a Burmese New Testament. In spite of repeated attacks of fever and dysentery, Judson believed on. When supporting friends decided he was not worthy of support because he could show so little fruit, he believed on. He wrote, "It requires a much longer time than I have been here to make an impact on a heathen people. . . . If we live some twenty or thirty years, they may hear from me again."

After eleven years, the tyrannical Burmese emperor imprisoned him for eleven months in a death house. At times he was manacled with three pairs of leg irons, at times with five pairs. He was driven barefoot over the burning sand at noon for several miles until his feet blistered, cracked open, and he left a blood-stain with each step on the sand. His feet were then put in stocks and raised higher than his head. The floor crawled with vermin. When Satan would taunt him about the slim prospects that seemed to exist for establishing Christ's church in Burma, Judson held on to the promises of God.

When his wife became so ill she could not nurse the baby, Judson was finally able to bribe the jailer to release him each evening so that he could carry his little withering baby from door to door to beg nursing Burmese mothers for a little of their own milk for his baby.

Yet they still believed God. Then his wife died; then their second baby died. After several years he remarried the widow of another missionary who had come out to join them. In time she died. Insurmountable odds, indescribable suffering, impossibility after impossibility, loneliness; and still Judson believed and pressed on until he died at sea en route home. To the end he believed and stood on the promises of God. During his only furlough back to America, street urchins, seeing God's presence on his face as he walked down the street holding the hands of his two surviving children, called him Mr. Glory Face. When he died, he left behind hundreds of graves of believers in Burmese soil, sixty-three churches, seven thousand baptized believers, and one hundred sixty-three missionary and Burmese co-workers. Today there is a church of some two million Burmese who name the name of Jesus as their Lord. There is no greater faith than that which lives on when all hope seems gone. What do you and I know of such faith?

7. *Measure your faith by your ability to praise in spite of.* Faith is not a fool. Faith is a realist. But faith praises God anyway. Faith can be hard pressed on every side but refuses to despair (2 Cor. 4:8). Faith can have a bleeding back, can have its feet shackled, but at midnight it will join Paul and Silas in singing praise to God. Measure your faith by your ability to smile when every one else is covered with gloom, by your ability to praise God when all others about you criticize and moan, by your ability to sing when many about you are in tears.

Faith is so God-centered that it lives "in spite of." Faith is so grounded on God's promise that it survives the tempest shock. It sings in spite of the failures of others. It perseveres in spite of threats and dangers. Faith marches out to battle singing praise to God, like Jehoshaphat, even when facing overwhelming enemy odds. "Give thanks to the Lord, for his love endures forever" (2 Chron. 20:20–22), and as faith praises God, God ambushes the enemy.

Yes, faith is a midnight singer. Faith is a Gideon-like victory shouter. Faith is a battlefield praiser of God. Faith is the victory that overcomes and praises as it overcomes. Measure your faith by your midnight song, by your Pauline, "I have faith in God," by your militant praise as you shout the name of Jesus and rout the devil. Measure your faith by praise.

God Can Do More

God has met you in the past and revealed His pow'r;
  You have known His miracle in the crisis hour.
You have witnessed in your life what the Lord can do;
  You have proved His promises in your life anew.

Thank the Lord for all He's done; He is still the same.
  He can do for you today more than all His fame.
Praise God for the hallowed past, sacred memories,
  But He longs to prove today new realities.

Use the mem'ries of the past to press on ahead;
  You can see new miracles as by Him you're led.
Thank the Lord, but, oh, beware; don't live in the past!
  All the Lord has ever done still can be surpassed.

Yes, His pow'r is just the same; this is still God's day.
  He today among us stands in our present way.
Lift your eyes in faith to God; prove His grace anew.
  God is waiting yet to show what His pow'r can do.

Wesley Duewel

10

MEASURE YOUR LIFE
BY HUMILITY

T hat person is greatest in God's sight who is least aware of his spiritual stature and who is least in his own sight. The Holy Spirit by the grace of God humbles a person without degrading him. When the Spirit exalts a person, He hides it in such beautiful naturalness that the person is unconscious of his spiritual greatness and is unconscious of his own humility.

John Flavel wrote, "They that know God will be humble; they that know themselves cannot be proud." Mountford added, "Let me truly feel that in myself I am nothing, and at once, through every inlet of my soul, God comes in, and is everything in me."

Thomas à Kempis assured us, "God walks with the humble; he reveals himself to the lowly; he gives understanding to the little ones; he discloses his meaning to pure minds, but hides his grace from the curious and proud."

Perhaps you would not agree fully with Augustine, but meditate on what he wrote: "Should you ask me what is the first thing in religion, I should reply, the first, second, and third thing therein—nay, all—is humility."

All of the Christian life is filled with paradox. You

are most truly spiritually alive when you are most truly
dead and crucified with Christ. You most fully and
eternally gain your life when you most deliberately,
lavishly, and joyfully give it to God and "lose" it for Him.
Humility is also one of the beautiful and costly paradoxes
of the spiritual life.

"Humble yourself before the Lord, and he will lift
you up" (James 4:10). Barclay translates this, "Come in
self-abasement to the Lord." And Berkeley words it,
"Take a low position before the Lord." The Amplified
Bible suggests that we should feel insignificant in the
presence of the Lord so that He can make our life
significant.

Spurgeon wrote: "The whole treasury of God will be
made over by deed of gift to the soul that is humble
enough to be able to receive it without growing proud
because of it. God blesses us all up to the full measure of
what is safe for Him to do. If you do not get a blessing, it
is because it is not safe for you to have one." Measure
your life by the extent to which it is safe for God to bless
you and answer your prayer.

It is not abject self-depreciation that the Bible
teaches. It is not ignominious groveling in the dust. That
would be a denial of your being the loved creation and
handiwork of God, of your being the purchased of God
by Christ's precious blood. Bible humility is fully consistent with your preciousness to God, with God's purpose
for you that you bring glory to Him, and your exaltation
through grace until you are seated with Christ in the
heavenlies (Eph. 2:6).

Measure your life by true Bible-taught humility,
Christlike meekness and gentleness (2 Cor. 10:1), and
godly self-forgetfulness as you pour out your life for
Christ and others. True Christly humility is attractive,

beautiful, and a tremendous Christian testimony. Are you known for Spirit-filled humility?

1. *Measure your humility by your sense of unworthiness of God's goodness and grace.* If you are truly humble, you will be constantly amazed that God is so good and gracious to you. God has already proved His love to you in numerous ways, but you do not take this for granted. You don't subconsciously feel God owes you favors because you are faithful to Him. No. Every time the Lord rewards you, deep gratitude wells up in your soul. You feel compelled to exclaim in the words Jesus taught, "I am an unworthy servant of the Lord; I am only doing what it is my duty to do" (Luke 17:10).

Adam Clarke was an early Methodist preacher who was truly ablaze for God and a co-worker of John Wesley. He mastered twenty languages. He was determined to use all his time for the glory of God. While others slept or spent their time casually, he studied, prayed, and worked. For twenty-seven years he used spare moments to write his great eight-volume commentary, which he finished on his knees. He was beloved by all his fellow ministers. Beginning in 1805, fourteen years following Wesley's death, Clarke was three times elected as president of the Methodist conference. The first time they elected him, he felt so unworthy that the ministers had to pick him up bodily and carry him to the platform and place him in the president's chair. But once there, he was greatly blessed and used of God as their leader.

The spiritually humble person is constantly aware of how indebted he is to God. He is like the man Jesus described who owed such an impossible debt that he could never hope to repay it (Matt. 18:23-27). How can one repay Calvary love? How can one help but be humbled before such a merciful, gracious, and good God? Measure your humility by your sense of unworthiness.

2. *Measure your humility by your sense of dependence upon God*. Jesus reminded us that apart from Him we can do nothing; He is the vine and we are the branches (John 15:5). What can the branches do without the vine? When you are great in humility, you are constantly aware that you are totally dependent upon God. The world and Satan constantly seek to deceive you and convince you to think that you can depend on your own wisdom, experience, or ability. Adam and Eve first fell into sin when they used their own common sense rather than to depend on God.

The more godly you become, the more gladly, completely, and constantly you rely on God. Christ is your source of wisdom. Christ is your source of power (1 Cor. 1:24). To you to live is Christ (Phil 1:21). To serve is to depend totally on Christ. You confess with Paul, "Not that we are competent in ourselves to claim anything for ourselves, but our competency comes from God. He has made us competent" (2 Cor. 3:5–6).

It has been well said, "There is no limit to what God can do for and through a person as long as that person does not touch God's glory." Measure your humility by your total reliance on God rather than on self, your total availability to God, and your total humble dependence on God. It can be fatal to God's power upon you if you begin to depend on your experience, if you feel you have acquired the "know-how," if you feel you have a method or message God is sure to bless. Never dare to rely on the past. Humble yourself anew and totally depend on God, on His guidance, anointing, and power.

Measure your life by your sense of your own nothingness, by your sense of your own complete failure apart from God, coupled with your rejoicing in the Lord's power and goodness. He who realizes his failure but is depressed by it is not humble; he is discouraged. But he who is absolutely nothing in his own eyes, but rejoices in and depends upon the ability and greatness of God, that one is truly great. His life is exceedingly precious in the sight of God. Oh, to be nothing, absolutely nothing so that God can be all and in all! There is no limit to the miracle God can do if we do not touch the glory.

3. *Measure your humility by your giving all the glory to God.* True humility gladly and constantly gives all credit to God. Spiritual humility makes you modest in accepting recognition of what you are and do. It studiously avoids and abhors all boasting and pride. It handles praise lightly and instantly passes it on to Jesus.

Measure yourself by your eagerness to decrease so that Christ may be all in all. Measure yourself by your willingness for others to receive the prominence while you are forgotten, for others to receive credit for what you have worked so hard to achieve. Measure yourself by your joy in working the hardest in the most obscure positions.

One of the reasons God could use D. L. Moody so greatly was Moody's humility. His close associate, Dr. R. A. Torrey, called Moody the humblest person he ever knew. Over and over while Moody preached he would look behind him on the platform, and, pointing to the younger men, would say with deep satisfaction, "There are better men coming after me." Moody preached, "The beginning of greatness is to be little, the increase of greatness is to be less, and the perfection of greatness is to be nothing."

Moses pointed out that God tests and proves us by humbling us (Deut. 8:2). Few people do well during the testing of their humility. Hence, God can use most people only to a very slight extent. When God tests a person to see if he takes to himself some of the credit and glory that belong to God alone, most people are found to be hungry for the praise of others.

That life is most mature in the sight of God that is most childlike. That service the greatest of all that most humbly becomes the slave of all. Only the humblest of persons can walk closely with God. Only the empty, thirsty persons can be filled, and only those who are absolutely nothing in their own sight can be entrusted with frequent miracles.

Measure your humility by your hunger for Jesus to get ever more glory, by your burning desire that His name be exalted. Measure your humility by your instant shuddering at the very thought of people giving glory to you that rightfully and fully belongs to God.

4. *Measure your humility by your holy inward response in the face of affront, indignity, and insult.* Measure your humility by your inner peace and joy when you are falsely accused, maligned, and slandered (Matt. 5:11–12). Measure your depth of humility by your consistent meekness, gentleness, and mildness when people ignore you, take advantage of you, or subject you to indignity. Measure your humility when for Jesus' sake you are dishonored and exposed to shame.

A favorite poem of Abraham Lincoln was by William Knox (1789–1825): "Oh Why Should the Spirit of Mortals Be Proud?" One day President Lincoln was told that one of his cabinet members, Edwin Stanton, had called him a fool. Stanton was brilliant, stubborn, and at times disrespectful. Lincoln humbly replied, "Well, if Stanton says I'm a fool, I guess I must be; for Stanton is a wise man, and is nearly always right in his decisions."

Paul said, "When we are cursed, we bless; when we are persecuted, we endure it; when we are slandered, we answer kindly" (1 Cor. 4:12–13). This is the beauty of Spirit-filled humility. This is "the unfading beauty of a gentle and quiet spirit, which is of great worth in God's sight" (1 Peter 3:4).

5. *Measure your life by your joy in doing anything and being anything for God and others.* Measure your life by your true joy in washing the feet of others (John 13:1–17), by your honestly preferring the honor of others to your own honor (Rom. 12:10). Measure your life by how constantly you "in humility consider others better than yourself" (Phil. 2:3). He who is most humble, most forgiving, most loving, most truly childlike is greatest in God's kingdom (Matt. 18:4).

Measure your lack of humility by your hunger for the praise of others, by your desire for position, by eagerness for recognition. Measure your lack of humility by your good opinion of yourself, by your habit of contrasting your own ability, efforts, or accomplishments with those of others. Measure your lack of humility by how often you feel hurt and slighted, by how deeply you feel resentment, and by how discouraged you become from the criticism of others.

Measure your lack of humility by how much you grumble about the treatment of yourself and how critical you feel of others, by how much you gossip about others. And remember, the measure of your lack of humility is the measure of your littleness in the sight of God.

The deeper your humility, other things being equal, the more God can use you. Holy total submission to God and holy humility make you great in the sight of God. Total dying to your own proud self-life, total crucifixion with Christ prepares you for God to use. After thirteen years of daily hungering and praying for God to send revival, Evan Roberts heard a message in which the minister said God needed to bend us in total submission before Him.

One night Evan became so hungry and desperate for God to work that in a prayer time in church he prayed over and over, "Bend me, bend me." He agonized in hunger of soul till the perspiration broke out. God "bent" him, crucified, cleansed, and filled him. Within a week revival broke out as he spoke to a small youth group and Roberts became God's instrument for revival across Wales in 1904–1905, and some 100,000 were powerfully converted and joined the churches. Harvest and awakenings spread to several other parts of the world. It was again the fulfillment of 2 Chronicles 7:14. It was again the proof that God works when His children purposefully humble themselves before Him.

Oh, the beauty of a truly humble soul! Oh, the power of a truly humble life! Oh, the exceeding greatness of God's power waiting to be revealed through those who are humble enough and small enough for God to use! Constant service with gracious humility, constant helpfulness with a sense of total nothingness, constant awareness of God's greatness and personal nothingness, constant forgetting of self with constant rejoicing in God as all-in-all—this is the measure of a soul truly great in the sight of the Lord. Measure your life—not by your position, not by your reputation, not by the kind words and praise that you receive. Measure your life by your happy and holy humility.

Pride Will Stop the Lord

Give all honor unto God;
 Spread His praise and fame abroad.
Take no credit for whate'er He does through you.
 Make His mighty workings known;
Praise belongs to Him alone.
 Give Him all the glory every day anew.

Oh, exalt His holy name;
 Do not touch His sacred fame.
Just remember by yourself you quickly fail.
 You are helpless; you are weak.
Daily you His grace must seek.
 It is only God Who through you can prevail.

Do not let pride enter in;
 All self-glory is a sin.
Pride will stop the Lord from working more through you.
 Humble yourself day by day;
Take the lowest, meekest way.
 When you're nothing, God new miracles can do.

Do not on yourself depend;
 Look to God His help to send.
Cast yourself upon Him totally for all.
 Glad thanksgiving to Him bring;
Give Him praise for everything.
 Then God's power ceaselessly on you will fall.

Wesley Duewel

11

MEASURE YOUR LIFE
BY OBEDIENCE

G od is measuring our lives, not by the measures and
standards of our culture or our age. He is measuring
them by our character and by our walk with Him.

God and His Word are intensely practical. All of the
great general principles in the kingdom of God are
illustrated and judged on the basis of the most specific
details. Nothing is left in the abstract. Everything is
brought down to the concrete situations in which believers live. God leaves no room anywhere for mere
nominal Christianity. Jesus' most scathing words were
not for the broken and degraded sinner who was con-
demned by society, but for the self-righteous and self-
deceived religious people whose lives did not prove their
claims to holiness, love, and relationship to God.

Jesus called such people fools, hypocrites, blind
guides, snakes, and whitewashed tombs. Seven times He
referred to them as blind. Three times He called them
vipers (Matt. 3:7; 12:34; 23:33). No condemnation seemed
too strong for those who failed to practice their professed
spirituality. This is in full harmony with His many other

statements, indeed, with the whole trend of Bible thought.

Perhaps the best illustration of this is the Bible emphasis upon obedience, an importance highlighted in both Old and New Testaments. The message of God is plain—measure your life by how much you obey—not by how much you know, by how much you do, by how much you read or hear, by how much you walk in the light, by how much you claim to have fellowship with God. Measure your life by what you actually do for God—not by what you intend to do. Measure your life by proofs in your daily living—not by your pious wishes.

Obedience to God—glad, full, and humble obedience—is God's ordained key to much that is vital in Christian life. Only the obedient Christian enjoys the constant and undimmed blessing and favor of God.

OBEDIENCE IS THE KEY

1. *Obedience is the key to cleansing and holiness.* There is no other way to maintain a holy life except to walk constantly in God's light. One step away from the light is a step away from the cleansing blood (1 John 1:7). Keep clean by obeying God.

2. *Obedience is the key to communion and fellowship with God.* It is as we walk in the light that we have fellowship with God and with God's children (1 John 1:7). Disobeying God quickly destroys fellowship.

Many people experience a "feeling of worship" as they sing choruses or hymns. Yet they continue in known disobedience of God. All such "feeling" and "experience" is deception rather than worship. Their sense of God's presence is emotion, not holy fellowship with God. God must be worshiped in spirit and in truth (John 4:24). To claim to have fellowship while deliberately disobeying

God is to walk in darkness. To claim fellowship with God while walking in darkness is to lie (1 John 1:6).

3. *Obedience is the key to spiritual understanding.* We must choose to do God's will if we would know God's truth (John 7:17). We understand the deep things of God only as we spiritually discern them (1 Cor. 2:14). That requires the help of the Holy Spirit whom God gives to the obedient (Acts 5:32). God has so much He longs to tell us, but the Spirit can teach us only as we are totally under His control, pleasing Him in total yielded obedience. Obedience is the key.

4. *Obedience is the key to confidence in prayer.* "Dear friends, if our hearts do not condemn us, we have confidence before God and receive from him anything we ask, because we obey his commands and do what pleases him" (1 John 3:21). Oh, how failing to walk in the light cripples our prayers! Oh, the unanswered prayers because the praying person is not living in full obedience to all of God's light! Obedience is the key.

5. *Obedience is the key to blessing.* Do you want to be blessed in your soul and blessed in all you do? Live in daily glad obedience to God. Seek and walk in God's light. James speaks of the one who lives in God's Word and walks in its light. "He will be blessed in what he does" (James 1:25).

God pours out His blessings on those who are eager and active in obedience, those who welcome new light, new guidance, new opportunities to bring glory to God. Many a Christian is dry in his soul and all too fruitless in ministry because he is so disobedient in practical matters like tithing, or in disciplining his life to find time for prayer. " 'Test me in this,' says the LORD Almighty, 'and see if I will not throw open the floodgates of heaven and pour out so much blessing that you will not have room enough for it' " (Mal. 3:10).

Obedience is the secret of all miracle. The opening of the Red Sea, the feeding of the five thousand, the raising of Lazarus, the outpouring of the Spirit on the Day of Pentecost—all were conditional on obedience. No promise is automatically fulfilled. Obey and you will receive.

6. *Obedience is the key to kingdom advance.* In one sense, God's kingdom advances on the feet, the words, the prayers, and all the obedience of God's children. A Christian poet has written:

> God has no hands but our hands
>   To do His work today.
> He has no feet but our feet
>   To lead men in His way.
>
> He has no tongue but our tongue
>   To tell men how He died.
> He has no help but our help
>   To lead them to His side.

God's kingdom advances through the Holy Spirit and the obedience of God's children. Both are indispensable. The Holy Spirit guides, anoints, empowers, protects, and uses us. But your obedience and mine are a cooperating all-essential part of God's kingdom strategy. He has ordained for the Spirit to work through us. Measure your value to Christ's kingdom by your obedience.

OBEDIENCE—THE MEASURE
OF SPIRITUALITY

Obedience is the measure of all spirituality.

1. *Measure your love for Christ by your total obedience to Him.* You are His friends if you do whatever He commands you (John 15:14), that is, anything less than one-hundred percent obedience is a proof of inadequate love. Do you desire a relation, a special closeness to Jesus?

Listen to what He says: "Whoever does the will of my Father in heaven is my brother and sister and mother" (Matt. 12:50).

Jesus says, "If you love me, you will obey what I command" (John 14:15) and "If anyone loves me, he will obey my teaching" (John 14:23). Any failure to walk in all the light, any lack of instant total obedience to the known will of God testifies to inadequate love or perhaps even spurious love. Measure how much you love God by how instantly and completely you obey Him in the smallest of details.

2. *Measure your faith by your obedience.* Faith without deeds is useless (James 2:20). To hesitate to give full and instant obedience proves a need for more faith.

3. *Measure your consecration by your obedience.* To obey is better than formal worship or to give sacrificially (1 Sam. 15:22). All religious ceremonies are valueless apart from obedience. To give all one's goods to the poor and one's own body as a martyr means nothing to God unless we have the love that acts in accordance with 1 Corinthians 13.

4. *Measure Christ's lordship in your life by your obedience.* Obedience is a measure of the extent of Christ's lordship over you. "Why do you call me, 'Lord, Lord,' and do not do what I say?" (Luke 6:46). What a searching question from Jesus. If Jesus were to speak to you in person today, would He have a comment about the measure of your obedience?

TWO FORMS OF OBEDIENCE

You are responsible for two forms of obedience: Obedience to God's general commands, and obedience to God's personalized commands. God's requirements, as taught in His Word, are for every person. You are responsible to obey them. You need no further guidance if it is in God's Word. That settles it. Forgiveness of others, restitution as far as possible of things wrongly taken, speaking no evil of others, children's obedience of their parents, tithing, moral purity—these are matters of obedience, according to God's Word, for every believer.

Some of God's requirements, on the other hand, are very personal. God may give you personal convictions about things. It is the obedience He requires of *you*, not of everyone. He may call you to missionary service, to special sacrificial giving to His kingdom, to a specific amount of time in prayer. He may not require these of others. They are God's personal guidance to you.

Abraham's obedience was tested in an intensely personal manner by the demand that he offer Isaac to God on an altar (Gen. 22). When God sent Philip on the road to Gaza to meet the Ethiopian eunuch, that was a personal obedience God required (Acts 8:26–40). So was the obedience of Ananias when God sent him to Saul of Tarsus while he was praying (Acts 9:10–19). Some of the prophets were given highly personal commands. Clear personal guidance becomes God's personal command to you, and God will reward you for your obedience.

HOW TO MEASURE YOUR OBEDIENCE

1. *Measure your obedience by how quickly you obey*. It is always pleasing to God that you prayerfully double-check whatever you understand to be God's will (see my book *Let God Guide You Daily*, Zondervan, 1988). However, once we know God's will, our obedience should be glad and instant. God may guide us to a new act of obedience at a particular point in the future.

2. *Measure your obedience by how gladly you obey*. God values our willing obedience more than our grudging

obedience. God rewards your joyful obedience more than your resentful obedience. Just as God loves a cheerful giver (2 Cor. 9:7), so He loves your cheerful obedience.

3. *Measure your obedience by how faithfully you obey.* When God assigns you a person to pray for or a form of service or blessing to others, be faithful day after day until God answers, blesses, or changes your assignment. Measure your obedience by your faithfulness in persever-ance, by your unwillingness to give up even when discouragement comes.

Mrs. Dorothy Clapp was an older Christian lady in one of the eastern American states. God led her to take as her prayer assignment a public high school down the street. Day after day, month after month, year after year she faithfully obeyed her prayer task. She prayed for God to save young people in that school. Then she began to pray that God would not only save them but send them to the ends of the earth. After twelve years of faithful praying, she began to pray for a mischievous young male student. She sent him a Gospel of John. For three more years she prayed, and at last God saved George Verwer.

Before long George had led two hundred other students to Jesus Christ. Some of them went to college and began to meet daily for prayer and went out together in evangelism. In 1957, three of them went to Mexico to evangelize during their summer vacation. By 1960, they were taking Christian youth also to Spain. By 1962, they had their first multination European campaign. By 1964, I had the joy of greeting George and the first Operation Mobilization group to India.

Now each year several thousand Christian young people from many nations join forces to evangelize, sell and distribute literature, and reach the nations for Christ. Operation Mobilization is reaching coastal ports by two gospel ships, training hundreds of youth each summer, and enlisting others in one- to two-year short-term service. Its "graduates" are strengthening the ranks of many Christian churches and organizations around the world.

It all can be traced back to one Christian lady who prayed for fifteen years for students at a high school. Only God has the total results recorded of her faithful obedience in prayer. In heaven, she is already rejoicing. But the full record will be tallied and her full reward will be given only at the judgment throne of Christ. There, before His assembled millions of saints, Jesus will call her forward, praise her for her faithfulness, and announce her great reward.

4. *Measure your obedience by how humbly you obey.* It is a privilege to obey God. It is an honor to obey Him, to be given the privilege of being used by God. Be careful, however, that you do not become self-confident or proud when God honors your obedience. Keep giving God all the glory. Keep low at Jesus' feet. Keep hidden behind His cross so that not you but Christ may be seen.

5. *Measure your obedience by your motive.* Beware of mixed motives. Do you obey because God demands it? Or do you obey because you want to please God (1 John 3:22)? Do you obey so as to be seen by people and receive recognition from them (Matt. 6:1)? Then you lose your reward. Do not seek to obey God so as to earn His favor, to give Him a kind of spiritual bribe in order that He may do what you want Him to do for you. Obey Him out of love, out of eager desire to please Him and give Him joy. Measure your obedience by your motive.

6. *Measure your obedience by how total it is.* We are not truly obedient to God when we walk in only part of God's light, when we choose what we will obey and what we will ignore because we want our own way. Measure your yieldedness, your consecration, your commitment to God

by how totally you obey and how faithfully you continue your obedience until God's goal is achieved.

If you have never made that total surrender of your all, your life, your ambitions, your plans, your present and your future, then this very moment hurry to the place of prayer and make a total surrender to Jesus of everything for all time and eternity. If you once made a total surrender but have since by self-will allowed reservations to enter into your consecration, if you are less yielded than you once were, run to the Cross and renew your total commitment. Calvary deserves your total commitment, your total obedience.

When Ruth Stam was a missionary child of seventeen in her parents' home in Africa, God began in her heart His call to the Tibetan people. She obeyed by reading everything she could about them. When she returned to the States for her education, she obeyed by equipping herself as best she could for missionary service. When she came out to India as a missionary, the door to Christian service in Tibet was closed, and her board assigned her to teach elsewhere. Later they put her in charge of teacher education. All this time she was obeying by equipping herself in every way she could. God's call to Tibetans remained constant, and even though the door remained closed, for ten long years she studied the Tibetan language as well as she could.

When the Dalai Lama, the living Buddha-god of the Tibetan people, fled to India, her mission transferred her assignment to Mussoorie, the very city assigned to the Dalai Lama by the government of India as his initial place of refuge. Prepared by years of obedience to God's call, Ruth Stam was God's person at the right place in the world at the right time for Him to use.

Her years of obedience in education and language study prepared her to become the education consultant for the Dalai Lama. She began to teach basic English classes to his people. Then she was asked to set up a teacher-training program for his people so that Tibetans could teach Tibetans. Ruth helped him place many Tibetan children in Christian schools, and a number of these found Christ as Savior.

For forty-four years, from before the Dalai Lama fled from Tibet to India, I have been praying daily for his salvation. He is still revered by almost all Tibetans as their living Buddha-god. God has brought him out of Tibet and given him a succession of contacts with Christian people. The long saga of God's grace reaching out to the Dalai Lama and to the Tibetan people is interwoven with the life of Ruth Stam and the obedience and prayers of many others that has now continued for more than fifty years. Your obedience now in praying for him and them can add to the completion of this story of God's grace and can lead to his conversion.

DO YOU REALLY WANT YOUR MEASUREMENT?

Do you want to measure the place God has in your life, the extent to which you are surrendered to Him, the extent to which your experience of God is real and not pious emotion? The extent to which it is not grounded on false hope? Measure it all by your obedience.

Many a person will come to the Judgment expecting great reward and learn that for them, too, the first are last and the last are first (Matt. 19:29–30). Many will claim to have prayed long prayers but will find that this only made their disobedience more abhorrent in the sight of God. Many will be able to point to visible results of their ministry and efforts, even to what seemed like miracles, only to be told that disobedience has robbed them of all claim of reward (Matt. 7:21–23).

Fellow Christians, this is a searching word of God. We are no better than our obedience. Measure your spiritual experience and your ministry by the immediacy, the joyfulness, and the totality of your obedience to the whole will of God in every detail of your daily life. Measure your life by your obedience.

Let Me Prove What Life Can Be

Lord, let me prove what life can be
   In all Your holy will.
I long each day more perfectly
   Your loving heart to thrill.
I want Your will by day and night;
   I dare not turn to left or right.
Let me live pleasing in Your sight
   And all Your plan fulfill.

I want to prove what You can do
   When You have perfect sway.
To Your life-plan I would be true;
   I only want Your way.
My will Your will alone shall choose;
   All other plans I must refuse.
I want You, Lord, my all to use;
   Lord, use me night and day.

Lord, let me prove the blessedness
   Of Your complete control.
Possess my human nothingness—
   My body and my soul.
Take all I am or e'er can be;
   Take all and use me utterly.
Fill me till men You only see
   And Your great name extol.

Lord, let me prove what life can be
   Lived out and out for God.
Let Your great glory visibly
   Through me be spread abroad.
Oh take me, use me for Your own;
   Be sovereign God on my heart's throne!
All glory be to You alone,
   My Savior and my God!

Wesley Duewel

12

MEASURE YOUR LIFE BY GUIDANCE

One of the great evidences of God's presence in a life is His guidance. The Spirit is actively interested and involved in your life as a believer. As much as your spiritual hunger, prayer, and obedience give Him the opportunity, He seeks to develop His fruit within your character. He seeks to make you salt, light, His witness, and a blessing to others. He seeks to bring glory to God through you every day.

The Spirit desires rapidly to mature His work of grace and the manifestation of Christlikeness in you. He longs to bring constant glory to God by your prayer, your witness, and the blessings flowing out from you. Therefore, He constantly seeks to guide and empower you.

It is important to the Spirit that your strength equal your days (Deut. 33:25) and that He empower you for all you do in His name (Acts 1:8). His resurrection power (Eph. 1:19–20) can be actively at work in you each day (Eph. 3:20). But such mighty workings in you require that the Spirit guide you daily. That is why God's promise is that He will guide you always (Isa. 58:11). It is so essential that God says being led by His Spirit is a proof that you are a child of God (Rom. 8:14).

It is normal for a child of God to be guided by the Spirit. It is abnormal to lack the experience of repeated guidance. God intends guidance to be so natural that you live a daily guidance lifestyle. Guidance is not merely for the spectacular crises of life. God's guidance should be as natural as God's enabling in prayer and God's empowering for holy living and for blessing others. God's guidance should be your daily experience if you are living up to His expectation.

God wants you to learn to recognize His voice (John 10:27). He wants you to follow His guidance because you know His voice (v. 4). His promise is, "I will instruct you and teach you in the way you should go; I will counsel you and watch over you" (Ps. 32:8). That is why Jesus' name is Wonderful Counselor (Isa. 9:6). That is why the Spirit is called *another* Counselor (John 14:16).

Your usefulness to God depends on your guidance by the Spirit and your empowering by the Spirit. The Spirit-filled Christian should be specially sealed by the guidance of the Spirit.

Anyone can make a mistake in guidance. But if you are constantly lacking in guidance and constantly making wrong decisions, you should search your heart to see why the Holy Spirit cannot guide you more clearly.

The Spirit-filled life should be marked by frequent occasions of your consciousness of His guidance and many more occasions when sometime after the event you see the evidence that without your realizing it at the time God did guide you. The blessed man of Psalm 1 delights and meditates in God's Word day and night, brings constant fruit, has unwithering leaves, and is marked by God's prospering and blessing whatever he does. Obviously, his life is one that is led by God.

If you are led by God, you find that each step leads to the next step. You do not have to retrace your way. Guidance often leads through impossibility to miracle, but it never leads through impossibility to defeat. The unguided person wastes a lot of time, effort, and expense by taking the wrong steps or taking the right steps at the wrong time. By his foolish steps, by his lack of tact, by his causing friction and misunderstanding, he proves that he is not being led by the Holy Spirit as much as he needs to be. He proves the emptiness of his life.

1. *Measure your nearness to God by your guidance.* The closer you live to God, the more you understand the things that please Him, and the more you share of His Spirit so that your touch at times becomes the touch of God upon others and your words become like words of God to them. The closer your fellowship is with God, the more He shares His plans and purposes with you. You become a friend of God like Abraham, of whom God said, "Shall I hide from Abraham what I am about to do?" (Gen. 18:17).

The more God starts you praying for things before He brings them to pass, the more He causes you to say the right word at the right time to influence and bless others; the more God whispers His intentions to you, the greater the proof that you are living near to the heart of God. Measure your nearness to God by your guidance.

2. *Measure your sensitiveness to God by your guidance.* If you are deaf to spiritual things, you will have difficulty understanding God even when He speaks in thunder tones. But if your spiritual hearing is good, you will hear His faintest whisper, saying, "This is the way, walk in it" (Isa. 30:21). If you are spiritually insensitive, you will seldom be conscious of God's guidance in prayer. You will be so absorbed in your own desires and interests that you will often lack the guidance of the Holy Spirit about

the precise needs for which He wants you to pray. Therefore, you will often lack the special help of the Spirit and His special faith that He inspires when you are praying according to His will. You will lack the joy of "praying through" in many of your prayer times.

If you are spiritually insensitive to God, you will find much of your praying is general. Receiving His guidance as to the specific details for which to pray, as to the very times when particular individuals need your prayer proves that you have a listening heart and that you are sensitive to the whispers of the Spirit. Measure your sensitiveness to God by your guidance in prayer.

3. *Measure your sensitivity to God by your guidance in the small details of your life and witness.* Has God guided you at times to a particular seat on a bus or train or in a public gathering so as to enable you to contact prepared hearts who need your witness? Does God guide you so that you know to whom to write letters of encouragement and blessing? Does God guide you for urgent need where you should give a special financial love gift to the Lord? Does God guide you so that you know which street to walk to save your time or to contact a heart in need? Does God guide you regarding which books to read or which portions of the newspaper to see important prayer topics and yet avoid wasting too much time with newspaper reading?

Does God guide you when to take a few moments in prayer so that you will be spiritually prepared before someone comes with an unexpected problem? Does God guide you about the proper approach to make to suit each individual you contact in your personal evangelism? Does God guide you concerning when to fast, when to set apart several hours of a night for prayer, when to rise several hours early for prayer? Measure your relationship to God by the constancy of His guidance in things great and small.

Do not measure your life by how busy you are, but rather by how much you are guided in what you do. It is not action, but guided action which brings results. Do not measure your life by how much you talk, but by how guided you are in what you say. Do not even measure your life merely by how much you talk to God, but take into account how much He says to you. A child that is close to its father is constantly guided by the father. A life that is indwelt by the Holy Spirit should repeatedly hear the voice of the Spirit. Of Him it is said, "He will guide you."

4. *Measure the frequency of guidance in your spiritual lifestyle.* The Holy Spirit delights to lead you into closer and closer fellowship with Jesus, to more and more of the fruit of the Spirit in your personality and character. Be thankful to God when you are aware of the deepening of your spiritual life. But this is often difficult to measure. However, you can know and measure more easily certain aspects of the Spirit's guidance in your spiritual life.

Measure the frequency with which the Holy Spirit gives you a special prayer burden for a person, a ministry, a family, group, or nation. Measure the frequency of a situation when He burdens you to pray at a specific time and then you later find that at that very moment a person or circumstance needed special prayer.

Measure the frequency with which the Spirit guides you to speak a word of encouragement to someone, to write a letter, or visit someone who is ill or spiritually needy. Measure the number of times the Spirit guides you to witness to a person. Measure the number of times the Spirit guides you to send a special offering or make a special financial investment in Christ's kingdom. Measure

the frequency of the Spirit's guidance in your spiritual life
and ministry.

On one occasion when I was speaking in Greens-
boro, North Carolina, I received a long-distance phone
call before the evening service from our OMS president,
Dr. Eugene Erny. He said a request had come for me to
fly to Korea for special meetings but that OMS was under
financial pressure and did not have the funds. At the close
of the service that night, Mrs. R. Z. Newton, a minister's
widow who worked as a counselor to help support
herself, came to me and asked me whether I needed $2000.
I had not announced my need. I replied, "No. I need
funds but not that much." "Well," she continued, "when
I got out of my car to come in to the service tonight, God
told me to give you $2000." The next morning she gave
me the money. I not only went to Korea but on to other
engagements from there, and God knew that for the
round trip I need the entire $2000.

Mrs. Newton explained to me, "You see, I am
accustomed to having the Lord tell me the exact amount I
am to give." She then related an occasion when the Lord
told her to give an elderly couple $3.75. She decided she
would put the exact amount in an envelope and deliver it
on her way home from work in the afternoon. But God
impressed her that she was to give it before she went to
work in the morning. She drove to the home of the
couple, honked her horn, and they came to her car. She
said, "Here is $3.75 God told me to give you this
morning." They praised the Lord and told her that that
was the exact amount they needed to have before noon
that day. They had just prayed for God to send it to them.

5. *Measure the frequency of the Spirit's guidance in more
secular or mundane activities.* The Holy Spirit loves you so
much that whatever is of interest or importance to you is
of concern to Him. He delights to guide you in your

travel arrangements so as to make them more satisfactory and to keep you safe. He desires to help you make wise expenditures that you will not regret, and that will perhaps save you money so you have more to give for Christ's kingdom. He may guide you to contact a specific person whom you had not planned to meet or did not know. That person may make a comment or have information that is of great importance to you.

The Spirit delights to guide you in your occupation so that you increase skill, avoid mistakes, discover better ideas, save time, or assist you in a hundred other practical details. Learn to listen to the gentle voice of the Spirit, to sense His quiet touch—whether to alert you, prompt you, check you, or restrain you.

Measure your guidance by the frequency with which you find the Spirit's guiding help in all the practical details of living. Let Him guide you to be a better parent, a better family member, a better citizen, a better employee, a better neighbor, or a better friend. Discover the romance of daily guidance.

6. *Measure your guidance by the frequency of those occasions when after an event is over you recognize that God truly guided you.* How often we do not discover until later how important a seemingly small detail actually is, or how significant a particular step is. Some of life's most important moments go unrecognized until later. Guidance is not just in the spectacular or dramatic moments. Often it is almost hidden in the ordinariness of our life and work.

What a delight to discover again and again that God motivated you or restrained you at just the right time, that you were guided to make just the right choice or decision. You hardly recognized at the time that you were being guided. You may not even have prayed at the specific moment. But as you look back, how glad you are that

God did guide you. You can gladly say, "Thank You, Jesus, for guiding me even when I did not realize it." Or, "Thank You, Jesus, for keeping me from making that mistake."

7. *Measure your guidance by the extent to which it becomes your daily lifestyle.* God wants to make His guidance so normal, so natural, so practical, and so constant that it becomes your spiritually natural lifestyle. Some Christians seem to make frequent mistakes in decisions large and small. They act almost unaware that God plans for His guidance to be their constant help in their daily living. Don't miss this aspect of your privilege as a child of God. It can give you constant joy to see God guiding you and to know that God is at work in your life. Read my book *Let God Guide You Daily.*

Guidance can be a constant joy as you sense the goodness and faithfulness of God. It will build up your trust and loving confidence in the Lord. Life will become a joyful romance as you expectantly look forward to new aspects and occasions of His faithful guidance. What can be more natural or delightful than for God, your Father, to guide you, His child, constantly (Isa. 58:11).

Measure your life by God's constant seal upon it. Measure your fellowship with God by His whispers to you. Measure your life not only by constant visible results but by God's constant loving guidance.

He Will Be Your Guide

In answer to your trusting pleas,
   From where you are to where He sees,
The Lord will be Your guide.
   He ever watches from above;
He plans and guides in constant love
   As you in Him confide.

He knows your prayers, your hopes, your dreams,
   And loving expectation beams
Upon His holy face.
   He feels responsible for you;
He joys to plan your future, too,
   And prove His loving grace.

He planned for you before your birth;
   He watched your every step on earth
And ruled and over-ruled.
   In all your life His love has shared,
And for your future path prepared
   As He your life has schooled.

The Lord will guide tomorrow, too;
   He Who has led will see you through—
His plan He will fulfill.
   Just praise Him for the days ahead;
The Lord will guide as He has led,
   And give you His good will.

Wesley Duewel

13

MEASURE YOUR LIFE
BY YOUR WORDS

B oth the Old and New Testaments repeatedly emphasize that God measures your life by your words. Often your speech is the most obvious and accurate measure of the reality and depth of your Christian experience, of the extent of your love to Christ, and the extent of your love toward others. Jesus Himself told us, "Out of the overflow of the heart the mouth speaks" (Matt. 12:34).

What you are is constantly revealed by what you say. Note carefully the flow of words of a person, especially during relaxed, unguarded moments, and you will get a picture of the quality of that person's mind, the quality of his character, the depth or shallowness of his Christian experience, and his strengths and weaknesses. The words reveal the person.

God makes very clear in His Word how closely heaven notices and records our words. This presents a tremendous opportunity to you as a Christian. God is keeping the record of all your loving words, helpful words, and encouraging words—plus the words you utter in prayer. You cannot possibly remember them all.

But God has the record, and all will add to your reward in heaven.

Again and again people have thanked me for a word that I had long since forgotten. But God used it at the time it was spoken to bring guidance, help, or some form of blessing. They can quote what I have forgotten. How much more heaven will surprise you by the way God has used your words. Why don't we invest more words of blessing in the lives of others?

But the judgment of our words, which is taught so clearly in the Bible, holds tremendous terror for the unsaved. They will reap results of all the sinful words they have ever spoken unless they truly repent and find forgiveness from God.

Words are important because they live on in their influence in other people's lives. Words have the potential of eternity in them. Once spoken they can never be recalled. They have tremendous power. They can be used for God, they can be wasted, or they can be used negatively, which always means that in some sense they accomplish Satan's purpose. Satan wants us to say the wrong thing or at least to waste our time and our words as much as possible.

What did Jesus mean when He said we would give an account for every careless word at the Judgment (Matt. 12:36)? Certainly it is easy to be careless with our words; they can damage far more than we intend. But once spoken, they are recorded for the Judgment (v. 37).

The Greek word used in this verse is *argos*. It means inactive, idle, unfruitful. Used of our words, *argos* means worthless, ineffective. It can include seemingly insignificant remarks. But they are not insignificant, for they reveal the condition of the heart. They are part of the almost unconscious overflow of what is within.

Words may show that we are empty-hearted, careless, foolish, critical, prejudiced, or sinful. Or they may reveal that we are thoughtful, considerate, caring, loving, good, prayerful, and holy. Our words speak loudly. They always speak even if we do not note our own words and what they reveal about us. Our words will speak most loudly at the Judgment.

Actually, the most casual, almost thoughtless words we speak sometimes reveal our true person more than our carefully prepared words. The hypocrite for a time can carefully frame his words to conceal his true feelings. But sooner or later his words will show who he really is. Words spoken almost unconsciously show true love, gentleness, and spirituality or a critical, grudge-bearing, angry heart. In them the real feelings are demonstrated.

The Bible indicates that people, angels, and God listen and note our words. Often the most significant words that reveal us are not the formal words of Christian testimony, which we give as a part of our service or Christian duty, but the natural outflow of words in the course of our normal living and in our unguarded moments.

Not only do God and people measure our lives in this world by our words, but our words will measure our lives at the Judgment. There is perhaps only one more searching measure of our lives—that is our thought life.

Undoubtedly, God measured Israel in the desert by various standards and found Israel spiritually lacking. But the measure most emphasized in Scripture is the grumbling words that God heard. Israel measured Miriam as a great woman leader, but God smote her with leprosy because of her jealous and critical words (Num. 12:1–15). "Don't grumble against each other, brothers, or you will be judged. The Judge is standing at the door" (James 5:9).

Have you ever realized how many of your grumbling, negative, or critical words are recorded in heaven?

Have you asked God's forgiveness for them? Are you disciplining yourself not to grumble or complain again about what God permits to occur in your life? Yes, God is listening to our words and especially to the words we speak of others.

Some lives are so full of graciousness and love that the moment anyone is mentioned the person has good words to say of that one. Other lives are filled with such bitterness, envy, and jealousy that a high percentage of their remarks are critical and disparaging ones. A sweet fountain cannot send forth bitter water (James 3:11). Love covers over a multitude of sins (1 Peter 4:8), but a carnal heart exposes and repeats a multitude of faults of others. Often when I hear Christians speaking among themselves, I feel like saying, in the words of Christ, "You do not know what kind of spirit you are of" (Luke 9:55, margin).

Have you not heard someone say, "Why, I did not know I said that," or, "I'm sorry; I did not mean to say that"? Do you see why your words are recorded for the Judgment? On the other hand, gracious words you scarcely notice or immediately forget also reveal your true heart. They also are recorded for God's reward at the Judgment Day. God is word-conscious. Are you?

God measures your life more by ten critical words spoken to your wife, husband, or friend and by words uttered negatively about an absent person than He does by a thousand words of public and formal Christian witness. Amy Carmichael said, "The absent are always safe among us." What a wonderful witness! Five cutting words spoken to or about another person will be of far greater importance at the judgment throne of God than ten thousand words of sermon, public prayer, or song.

The Lord listens when His children speak to one another (Mal. 3:16). Some committee meetings that have been counted of great value to the kingdom of God by official records have given God an entirely different measure of the individuals who argued and spoke in a carnal manner. A few words sowing suspicion and discord, spoken from a selfish heart, measure the speaker immediately as an abomination in the sight of God (Prov. 6:16, 19).

God measures all our words—the words that build up and are constructive and the words that wound and are destructive. The Bible lists both kinds of words, with the book of Proverbs citing many: hasty words (29:20), rash words (13:3), harsh words (15:1), and words that separate even close friends (17:9). It also lists timely words (15:23), healing words (12:18; 15:4), words aptly spoken (25:11), pleasant words (16:21, 24), and gracious words (22:11). In addition, Paul speaks of empty words (Eph. 5:6).

If you are filled with the Spirit of God, you cannot but speak things God is revealing to you. The abundance of your heart will repeatedly overflow. If you are filled and thrilled with love for Christ, you will evidence your joy in Christ in a thousand little expressions from your mouth. But if you are filled with the spirit of the world, if you are not merely in the world but of the world, you will show where your treasure and your heart are in a thousand ways in your conversation.

Take your choice. Words can show your Christian love. Words can help people to Christ. Words can build up and strengthen your fellow Christians. You can fill your conversations with words about the Lord, and as you do your heavenly Father will be your constant listener. The record of your love, as proved through your words, will be recorded in heaven. This will make you a precious treasure to God and will bring you abundant reward (Mal. 3:16–18).

Or you can fill your hours with trivial words, mere chitchat, words that consume your time and keep you from accumulating all the potential reward of the time you wasted. Or, worse still, your words can wound, hinder, and bring you embarrassment and shame when they are reported before Christ's judgment throne at the final day. They will be burned up like wood, hay, or straw (1 Cor. 3:11–15). If it is thus judged by God, you may be saved by God's grace, but you will lose forever some of your potential reward.

Measure your life by your words and conversation:

1. How many times does the Spirit prompt you to speak to someone, or guide you in speaking words of blessing?

2. What percent of your words are loving, helpful, and encouraging to others?

3. What percent of your comments about other people are positive and appreciative rather than negative?

4. What percent of your conversations are cheerful, full of faith, and hope inspiring rather than gloomy, fearful, and hesitant?

5. Into what percent of your longer conversations do you bring a reference to Jesus, God's goodness, or Scripture?

6. Do your conversations reveal you to be gracious and sociable or silent and withdrawing? Do they reveal you to be a warm person who constantly dispenses blessings or a severe and morose person who scatters gloom? Are you a quiet and cheerful person or a loud and boisterous person? Are you a good listener or an excessive talker? Are you able to maintain confidences or are you a frequent gossip and self-centered? Are you a promoter of unity or a divisive person?

7. What percent of your conversations are constructive and edifying?

One day on a Christian college campus a professor startled me by saying, "I'm here today because of what you said to me that day." "What day?" I asked. I had absolutely no recollection of the occasion or what I said. I am still almost shocked how many Christian young people have been guided by that faculty member since that occasion! What if I had not been guided and anointed in what I said on that forgotten occasion!

On a Sunday morning years ago at a church I happened to visit on a free day while I was home from India, I found they were having special meetings. At the close of the service the song evangelist came and greeted me by name. I did not remember having met him before. He said, "I'll never forget what you said to me that night. It was a turning point in my life." To this day I cannot recall the event or what we talked about. Since that time he has become the international radio voice of his denomination. Later, he became one of the main leaders of the worldwide ministry of his denomination. What if I had failed him! What if I had not been guided and anointed in whatever I said!

Christ's judgment day can have wonderful surprises and rewards for you for words you don't even remember speaking. Or it can be a shocking revelation of words you failed to speak or of words you spoke that hindered other people and hindered Christ's kingdom. Heaven is recording your words. Are you watching and measuring your words? God is constantly measuring them.

Measure your life by your words. People have already been measuring you that way. Angels have been recording your words for the final day of measurement and judgment, that you may receive your reward or loss. God has been measuring your life by your words. Dare you?

Christian, Guard Your Tongue!

God pours refreshment on your soul
  When on your knees you tarry.
He waits to touch and make you whole
  And lift the load you carry.
His heav'nly dew in grace descends
  In blessing upon blessing;
But wait—how much on you depends!
  This point we must keep stressing:
Christian, guard your tongue!

How much of blessing dissipates
  Through frequent careless talking!
How oft you rise to heaven's gates
  As with your Christ you're walking,
And then so quickly lose it all
  By words that were not needed!
How oft you wish you could recall
  The darts your lips have speeded.
Christian, guard your tongue!

The tender Spirit of your God
  From your words oft is grieving;
The blessing He would shed abroad
  How oft you stop receiving!
You lose the freshness of His touch;
  You fail in pray'r to tarry
Because you simply talk too much
  With words unnecessary.
Christian, guard your tongue!

How difficult it is to speak
  At length without complaining!
How easy does God's blessing leak
  When you lack His constraining!
When on you gossip carelessly
  In almost endless chatter,
When on you speak so prayerlessly
  Of things that do not matter!
Christian, guard your tongue!

Lord, help us watch each careless word;
    Let nothing e'er be spoken
That could grieve others if they heard
    Or leave their spirits broken.
How easy to talk by the hour
    And grieve your Holy Spirit,
To lose by wordiness the pow'r
    That we so sorely covet!
Help us guard our tongues!

Lord, place a watch upon our lips.
    Our speech with grace, Lord, season.
Preserve us from unguarded slips
    And words without a reason.
Give us more quietness of heart
    And teach us meditation.
Help us to set our tongues apart
    In fullest consecration.
Savior, guard our tongues.

                                    Wesley Duewel

14

MEASURE YOUR LIFE
BY YOUR THOUGHTS

There is no more searching measure of your life than your thoughts. It is one of the easiest tests to apply to yourself. Who you really are is demonstrated in your thoughts. Your thoughts express your inner person— your motives, desires, aims, feelings, and the principles that govern your life. Your thoughts and your will are closely related. Your thoughts and your will express and control your soul.

God constantly notes and evaluates your thoughts. To a godly, Spirit-filled person this is usually a comfort and joy. You are glad He knows you through and through. You have nothing to hide. You are totally open to God. Listen to the satisfaction and openness in David's prayer in Psalm 139, "O LORD, you have searched me and you know me. . . . You perceive my thoughts from afar. . . . Before a word is on my tongue you know it completely, O LORD" (vv. 1–4).

How gladly David opens his heart totally to God as he concludes the psalm. "Search me, O God, and know my heart [also translated 'thoughts']; test me [also translated 'probe me'] and know my anxious thoughts. See if there is any offensive way in me [also 'watch lest I follow any path that grieves thee,' NEB; or 'point out anything you find in me that makes you sad,' LB; or 'see whether there is any baneful motive within me,' BERK.]" (Ps. 139:23–24).

What does the Bible mean by your thought? It cannot refer to a momentary thought that flits through your mind when you unexpectedly hear or see something. That involved no choice on your part. You cannot be alive and avoid the sights, words, and sounds about you or the tempting thoughts that Satan injects into your mind like a flaming arrow (Eph. 6:16). It is your reaction to these that God notes.

You have constant choice in how you respond to the thoughts that are forced upon you by life. It is when you pause to consider, when you continue to think about them, when you welcome them and come back to them again and again that God evaluates you. When you entertain thoughts, give consideration to them, and especially when you cherish or nurture them, you become worthy of praise or blame. These are the thoughts that reveal you and further influence you. Such thoughts and meditation reveal your heart.

Holiness of life begins in the cleansing, empowering work of the Holy Spirit in your "heart." Your heart, as expressed in your thought life, is the fullest expression of your real self.

No other person can fully know you or measure you because no one else fully knows your thoughts. God does not merely measure your words and activities. He is constantly observing and recording your thoughts. This is an unspeakable blessing for a Spirit-filled Christian who walks in God's light and is hungry to please God.

Heaven knows you by your thoughts. Even when Jesus was on earth He knew what people were thinking

(Matt. 9:4). Your thoughts comprehend all of the real "you." They include your desires, your prayers, your attitudes, your purposes and goals, your joys, your loves, your faith, your determination, your intent, your motives. All you are and all you do is expressed by your thoughts.

Almost always your actions express only a part of your motive, desire, or inner nature. You may love God or others either more or less than you express. Your words are so very important. But of even deeper importance are your thoughts.

Thank God, fellow Christian, that the Holy Spirit is an active, constant, perfect discerner of the thoughts and motives of your heart (Heb. 4:12–13). Thank God that you will be rewarded for your motives, holy hungers, deepest godly longings, for your inner commitment, not only for what you manage to express.

When God sees you, He sees more than your words and actions. He sees you through and through. God's grace is given to transform you through and through says 1 Thessalonians 5:23. What holy, thrilling surprise and joy at the judgment seat of Christ when longings that characterized your heart-cry, your very soul, receive God's holy commendation, when your loving thoughts for God and man, long forgotten, are revealed and rewarded.

An example of this is given by God's revelation through the prophet Malachi. Speaking of God, he wrote, "A scroll of remembrance was written in his presence concerning those who feared the LORD and honored his name [in Hebrew: 'thought upon his name']" (Mal. 3:16).

Both Old and New Testaments illustrate the importance of your thought life and that your thoughts are the measure of your person. "As he thinks in his heart, so is he" (Prov. 23:7, NKJV). "Out of the overflow of the heart the mouth speaks" (Matt. 12:34). But always much that is thought and entertained in the heart is never spoken. A person's words may cover up his real thoughts.

The heart itself can be so deceitful that you know it only by your thoughts. "I the Lord search the heart and examine the mind, to reward a man according to his conduct" (Jer. 17:10). You may need the Holy Spirit to help you recognize how your thoughts appear to God. He is called "he who searches our hearts" (Rom. 8:27).

You are no greater than your thoughts, no more holy than your thoughts. You are no more loving, humble, or patient than your thoughts. You are what you choose to think upon. God's angels know you by your thoughts, and one day at Christ's judgment throne the world will know you by your thoughts (Rom. 2:15–16).

A child is known by childish thoughts and a mature person by the maturity of his thoughts (1 Cor. 13:11). The child not merely delights to think on childish interests, he does not know how to discipline his thoughts. He thinks about what he sees and forgets quickly other things. Spiritual childishness and immaturity is shown in the same way. No Christian dare be content until he has brought every thought into captivity to make it obedient to Christ (2 Cor. 10:5). Then "whatever is lovely, admirable, excellent or praiseworthy," these will be the things on which the mature saint thinks (Phil. 4:8).

Measure your life by the extent to which you think of praiseworthy things about people and the extent to which you remember and brood upon unfavorable things about people. Measure your soul by the extent to which you think loving and appreciative thoughts of people and the extent to which you think critical thoughts and condemn other people in your heart, including those who work with you or work for you.

Measure your soul by the memories you cherish about former neighbors, coworkers, and friends. Do you remember the beautiful, the lovely, the praiseworthy? Or do you remember the faults, the failures, and the sins? Measure the extent to which you have forgiven others and trust to be forgiven by the Lord to the extent to which you forgive and forget the sins of others (Matt. 6:14–15).

Measure the extent to which you are one with Christ by the readiness with which you forget material things and lovingly think of Him, by the joy with which you turn from thoughts of people to thoughts of Him, by the constancy with which your loving thoughts of Him occupy your free moments.

Measure your faith by the extent to which your heart is filled with thoughts of joyful expectation, trust, and praise. Measure your lack of faith by the extent to which you have anxious thoughts about the tomorrows, by the amount of time you spend fearing and worrying, by the number of things that you let trouble your thoughts. Measure your faith by the extent to which the peace of God rules your heart (Col. 3:15) and by how filled your mind is with praise and thanksgiving to God.

Measure your humility or lack of humility by the extent to which you remember and repeat in your mind the praises other people give you. Measure it by the extent to which you hunger for and are disappointed if you do not receive praise from others. Measure your lack of humility by the extent to which you remember your own good deeds and forget the good deeds of others. Measure your pride by the extent to which you mentally contrast the poor performance of others with your own actions.

This measure can be applied quickly and easily to any aspect of your spiritual life. Measure your worship of God by the greatness, joyfulness, and constancy of your thoughts of Him. Measure your love of Scripture by the amount of Scripture you have stored up in your heart and the extent to which you meditate upon it. Measure your watchfulness for your Lord's return by the extent to which His coming motivates your actions and is the subject of your prayers.

It is out of the abundance of your heart and your thought life that your words come forth. It is out of the abundance of your heart that your life is built. God measures your acts and words, but above all He measures your thoughts. He measures and rejoices to see your reaction to thoughts that are repulsive to you and that you put from you as quickly as possible. He measures the thoughts that are your joy, that you cherish and meditate upon over and over. From this He knows the extent to which you hate what He hates and love what He loves.

Perhaps one of the most uplifting examples of a Christian whose thought life was saturated with God's presence and God's love was John Fletcher, the coworker of John Wesley, who was said by Wesley to be the godliest person he had ever known. Fletcher had been a person with a strong temper, and he often lay on the floor in agony of heart and pleaded and prayed for hours and sometimes the whole night to be delivered. He received an overwhelming experience of being filled with the Spirit. God manifested His love to and in Fletcher until he feared he would die of the glory.[1] Wesley testified that from then on for more than thirty years, until Fletcher died, "no one ever saw him out of temper, or heard him utter a rash expression."[2]

It is said that following his encounter with the Holy Spirit, Fletcher's every word seemed to be prayer, praise, or spiritual truth. "Every word that fell from his lips appeared to be accompanied with an unction from above." He seemed to live and think and talk in the Spirit. He was called "an angel of a man."[3]

Fletcher was called "apostolic" in his preaching. Often the buildings could not hold the crowds, and people stood outside listening in through windows. For three years he was top official of Trevecca College in Wales, the school founded by Wesley's friend Lady Huntingdon. The headmaster under Fletcher said, "He was received as an angel of God." When Fletcher was present, students laid aside everything to listen to him. He spent hours on his knees praying for the students. Once he was so overwhelmed with the Spirit's fullness and power that, like Moody when he was Spirit-filled in Boston, Fletcher called out, "O my God, withhold thy hand, or the vessel will burst!"[4]

Fletcher and his wife "kept heaven in their home,"[5] continually sang doxologies, were constant in prayer and unwearied in labor for souls. John Wesley frequently stayed in their home and wanted Fletcher to be his successor, but Fletcher died many years before Wesley.[6]

Fletcher's thoughts were so full of prayer and praise that his greeting when meeting one of his friends was "Do I meet you praying?"[7] Often he would drop on his knees as he entered a home and pray for all present. If anyone spoke an unfavorable word about anyone, his usual reply was, "Let us pray for him."

At times he would get so hungry for prayer that while talking to others he would say, in the words of Matthew 26:36, "Sit ye here, while I go and pray yonder" (KJV). His greatest joy was to spend time in his prayer room. He was constantly giving thanks to God. "His heart was always in a grateful frame, and it was his chief delight to honor God by offering his praise and thanksgiving. Frequently he has broken out in a strain of holy rejoicing." He was said to labor constantly "to bring every thought into captivity to the obedience of Christ."

As Fletcher lay dying, his thoughts were filled with

God. Again and again he said, "God is love! It fills me every moment! God is love! Shout! Shout aloud! Oh, it so fills me that I want a gust of praise to go to the ends of the earth!" When he no longer had strength to speak, someone asked him to raise his right hand if Jesus was still present with him and heaven was opening before him. He raised his hand.

It is your thought life that molds you into Christ's image or into the image of the world and Satan. It is your thought life that proves the extent to which the Holy Spirit fills you. It is in your thought life you respond to the work of the Spirit that can lead to the transfiguration of your whole character and soul, into the whole measure of the fullness of Christ (Eph. 4:13).

Measure your life by your thoughts, for this is the measure Satan applies, this is the measure the angels of God apply, and this is the measure of the Holy Spirit Himself (Heb. 4:12). Measure your life by your thoughts today and you will have nothing to be ashamed of when the motives of your heart are revealed on the judgment day of Christ (1 Cor. 4:5). Measure your life by your thoughts, and if you stand approved you will have confidence before God (1 John 3:21–22). Measure your life by your thoughts, and humble yourself in the sight of God that He may renew your mind and may mold you according to His will (Rom. 12:2).

Dr. Edwin Orr wrote a song that echoes Psalm 139:23–24:

> Search me, O God, and know my heart today;
>   Try me, O Savior, know my thoughts, I pray.
> See if there be some wicked way in me;
>   Cleanse me from ev'ry sin and set me free.

Notes

[1]James Gilchrist Lawson, *Deeper Experiences of Famous Christians* (Anderson, Ind.: Warner, 1911), 199. Wesley's estimate of Fletcher is cited also in McLeister, p. 211 (see note 5 below).

[2]Ibid., 200.

[3]Ibid., 198.

[4]Ibid., 198–99.

[5]Clara McLeister, *Men and Women of Deep Piety* (Cincinnati: God's Bible School and Revivalist, 1920), 191.

[6]Ibid., 192.

[7]Ibid., 205.

15

MEASURE YOUR LIFE BY YOUR INVESTMENTS

L ife is an investment. God planned it that way. For every hour we sow in our earth life, there will be millions of years of reaping during eternity. No life will ever end. Once we are conceived in our mother's womb, we will never cease to exist. Death does not end existence. Nothing that a person can ever do can shorten his existence or cause it to end.

The Bible calls our life on earth a time of sowing. Ultimately only two kinds of sowing are open to us. We can sow righteousness, and if we do we will reap a "sure reward" (Prov. 11:18), "unfailing love" (Hosea 10:12), and "eternal life" (Gal. 6:8).

Or, we can sow sin (Prov. 22:8) and we will reap trouble, destruction (Gal. 6:8), and "everlasting destruction"; and we will be eternally "shut out from the presence of the Lord" (2 Thess. 1:9), which means "eternal judgment" (Heb. 6:2), and eternal fire (Jude 7), which is "the second death" (Rev. 20:14), that is, existence in eternal destruction and death.

You begin to reap some of your life's investments already in this life (John 4:36). You can invest kindness, helpfulness, and good deeds, and often begin now to receive rewards of a good name, respect, and appreciation, plus the joy of a good conscience and a sense of God's blessing and favor. A wonderful example of this is Florence Nightingale who, following God's call at the age of sixteen and God's continuing guidance against unbelievable odds during the Crimean War, faced scorn, insult, and rebuff from army medical leaders. But in spite of their opposition, she was able to revolutionize the British army's medical procedures and provisions, and introduce a new system of women nurses. She was the founder of modern nursing and had a great influence in the organization of the Red Cross. She not only saved the life of multiplied thousands, but transformed hospitals in Europe, Asia, and Africa. Ridiculed and opposed by family, the medical profession, and society, hers became one of the most respected names in history. Though weak in body, she invested her life from her teen years to fulfill God's call to her.

Even the unsaved person can invest in some helpful ways, and he will thus have less sin to reap eternally. It will not cause him to earn or merit salvation, for that is God's free gift, which is given according to God's clearly stated conditions. It will not cause him to reap in heaven, for without salvation he does not go to heaven. By doing good, the sinner gets his only rewards here in this life, although he will have fewer sins to give account of before God at the judgment and on throughout eternity.

The Christian makes a double investment and reaps double blessings—both here on earth (comparatively speaking, the smaller reward) and in eternity (the incomparably great reward). Reaping here is only for a short time. Reaping in eternity is unending.

The person who has money to invest for God but fails to invest it is one of earth's fools. Every person has a life to invest, time to invest, abilities to invest, money and possessions to invest. To fail to invest them according to God's will is to be a fool in eternity. We do not all have the same length of life, or the same abilities, possessions, or opportunities. But if we use to the full what we have, investing all according to God's will and for God's kingdom, we will all receive equal commendation from God (Matt. 25:14–23).

The Bible teaches that we will reap what we sow and according to the extent of our sowing. "Do not be deceived: God cannot be mocked. A man reaps what he sows. . . . Let us not become weary in doing good, for at the proper time we will reap a harvest if we do not give up. Therefore as we have opportunity, let us do good to all people" (Gal. 6:7, 9–10). "Remember this: Whoever sows sparingly will reap sparingly, and whoever sows generously will also reap generously" (2 Cor. 9:6). It is possible to invest life so that we are "not rich toward God," said Jesus (Luke 12:21). This obviously means we can invest our lives so that we will be "rich toward God." We are to "provide purses" for ourselves that will not wear out, "a treasure in heaven that will not be exhausted" (Luke 12:33).

Financial investment for God and His kingdom is important, but for everyone the opportunities for nonfinancial investment are greater. God's kingdom advance is in continuous need of financial support. But the need for investment in ardent intercession is overwhelmingly greater. And the need for investment of loving words and deeds never ends. Everyone is limited in resources and unable financially to support the ministry of the church and Christian organizations as fully as he would like. But no one need be limited in the investment of loving prayer.

Measure your life by your investment of love. How

much love do you invest in the church? Do you truly rejoice in every new person coming to Christ? How much time are you investing each day in praying for the unsaved? How many unsaved people are on your daily prayer list? Measure your love by the amount of time you pray for your pastor, the youth of your church, the elderly, and the unsaved. Measure your life by the amount of love you invest in others during your normal activities.

In the late nineteenth century a humble, Spirit-filled woman lived in Crab Orchard, Kentucky, and kept the tollgate on a Kentucky road. Mary McAfee invested her life for Jesus each day by a happy smile, a cheerful greeting, a constant prayer for all those who passed through the tollgate. She repeatedly brought the Lord into her greetings to the travelers and often shared her testimony with them. A newspaper reporter for the Louisville, Kentucky, *Courier-Journal* heard of her and went to Crab Orchard to ask her the secret of her radiant joy. He published her story of how she had been filled with the Spirit and how her life had been transformed.

By God's providence, a copy of that issue of the paper reached the hands of a minister in the state of Mississippi. He was hungry for a deeper life in God but did not know to whom to turn to guide him. He traveled six hundred miles by train to meet Mary McAfee and ask her the secret of her joy. She prayed with him, and he spent three days praying and looking to God. He was wonderfully filled with the Spirit and set aflame on the third day of his conversation with this humble woman.

The minister became an evangelist who held many series of revival meetings across the South. Hundreds were saved, and others were called into evangelism. In eternity the full record of the humble tollgate keeper will astound her—all because she invested love, joy, and blessing as she did her daily work.

Measure your life by your investment of love and time in your nation. How many national leaders do you pray for each day (1 Tim. 2:1–3)? Do you pray daily for God to restrain sin and evil in your nation? for God to stop child abuse? wife abuse? youth gangs? the liquor and drug menace? the filth in the media and entertainment industry? How much love and prayer are you investing in your nation?

You can make a difference in your nation by large investments of prayer. Ezra wept for Israel, and so did Nehemiah. David wept for his nation. Jeremiah had a broken heart and invested constant prayer for Judah. The survival of the Jews and the coming of Christ through the Jewish nation were made possible by the prayer investment of these and of Isaiah, Hezekiah, Jehoshaphat, and of many hidden intercessors right down to the time of Anna and Simeon (Luke 2:25–38).

Every investment of your time and love in prayer for revival, for world harvest, for the return of Jesus is an eternal investment (1 Cor. 16:22). Every investment of loving concern as you pray for the unsaved, for those injured, ill, lonely, and depressed is an eternal investment. As surely as God is in heaven, if you are investing yourself and your prayer in these you will reap eternal reward. As sure as God is in heaven, if you go through your hurting world with eyes too blind to see and a heart too loveless to pray, you will be an eternal loser (1 Cor. 3:15).

Measure your life by your investment of tears for others and for the advance of the Gospel and the salvation of the nations. Measure your life by how deeply you hunger for the salvation of the unsaved, by how fully you grieve for those who experience tragedy, by how your heart goes out to those needing your prayer. When you share Jesus' longing and heart-cries, your life extends to Godlike dimensions. You are adding eternal significance to your hours. You are great in the sight of God. "Those who sow in tears will reap with songs of joy. He who goes out weeping, carrying seed to sow, will return with songs of joy, carrying sheaves with him" (Ps. 126:5–6).

Jeremiah invested tears in what seemed a hopeless cause as Israel continued to reject his pleadings and warnings. "O my Comforter in sorrow, my heart is faint within me. Listen to the cry of my people. . . . Since my people are crushed, I am crushed; I mourn, and horror grips me. . . . Oh, that my head were a spring of water and my eyes a fountain of tears! I would weep day and night for . . . my people" (Jer. 8:18, 21; 9:1).

Jeremiah is often called the weeping prophet. He did weep as he interceded for his people. Do you? But tears cannot always flow from your eyes. What you need more than weeping eyes is a weeping heart. Are you investing heart tears for those for whom you intercede? The more you invest, the greater your eternal reward!

But let Jeremiah continue: "If you do not listen, I will weep in secret because of your pride; my eyes will weep bitterly, overflowing with tears" (13:17). If God gives you tears in public, He can use them. But the main place for your investment of longing intercession and intercessory tears, like Jeremiah, is in private. If you love deeply enough, if you are constantly faithful in investing hungry-hearted intercession, you can be eternally rich in invested Christlike tears. Are you rich in tears?

Measure your life by the hungers of your heart. Heart-hunger is a costly but godly investment. The more you share the heartbeat of Christ, the more you love with His longings and intercede with His pleadings, the more you will know with Paul "the fellowship of sharing in his sufferings" (Phil. 3:10).

What does it mean to invest your life as a living sacrifice? How can your body, your mind, your holy emotions, your surrendered will be invested day by day for eternity? Such costly outpouring of your whole soul and being is itself a spiritual worship of God as acceptable and pleasing to God as the worship of the seraphim (Rom. 12:1–2; Isa. 6:3).

Henrietta Mears, at the age of five, was beautifully led to the Lord by her godly mother. When she was ten, she and her little cousin called themselves "the Willing Workers"—"to do good for unfortunates." Repeatedly in her childhood she asked for the pastor to come and pray for her when she became ill, and she was repeatedly healed of a punctured eye, frequent nosebleed, and severe and painful crippling muscular rheumatism. She learned to trust God in everything.

In her teens she learned from her godly mother to witness, distribute New Testaments on the streets, and lead people to Christ. She prayed for weeks for God's power to fill her and use her. Then one day she realized that she must only reach out to God and by faith receive the Holy Spirit's fullness. From then on all of her life was marked by the leading, empowering, and anointing of the Holy Spirit.

When she was twelve years old, Henrietta began to invest her time in teaching Sunday school classes. On through high school and college she kept investing herself. She became tremendously effective with teenagers. On one occasion they decided to form a new Sunday school class. She and her sister scoured the neighborhood house to house, and the first Sunday they started the class with fifty-five new girls. Then she started a class for young married women.

A visiting minister, who pastored a small church in Hollywood, insisted that she come to California and assist him. There she continued investing herself and was the key person in development of the Christian education department of First Presbyterian Church of Hollywood. Over the years she became God's special agent in the lives of hundreds of young people. Many of these became greatly used by God.

She continued to invest herself at Forest Home Conferences with various Christian groups in the Hollywood area. The investment of her love and life continues to bear fruit today in the lives of hundreds of people, including many well-known names, such as Dr. Louis Evans, Jr.; Dr. Richard Halverson, chaplain of the United States Senate; Dr. William Bright, who founded Campus Crusade for Christ; Dr. Billy Graham; Lillian Dickson, famous missionary to Taiwan, and others. She had a key role in the Hollywood Christian group, which won many actors and athletes to Christ. She formed Gospel Light Publications, which has developed a worldwide ministry in the production of literature for Christian education. All of these achievements are the outflow of Henrietta Mears's life investment from childhood on. She continued to invest herself to her last day on earth, March 18, 1963.

When you pour out your soul in devotion, you are investing and qualifying for a place eternally close to the heart of God. Daniel identified with His people with mighty and faithful Christlike intercessions for God's will to be fulfilled on earth. He pleaded for them. "I turned to the Lord God and pleaded with him in prayer and petition, in fasting" (Dan. 9:3). He mourned for his people for three weeks with partial fasting as he kept up his imperial duties as prime minister. He kept crying out to God in longing intercession, at times on his face before God. (Note: "stand up," v. 11.)

Gabriel was twice sent to Daniel to help answer his prayer. Gabriel called him "highly esteemed" (10:11). In Hebrew this word means greatly desired or greatly delighted in. If you invest your love, your time, your very soul in such deep intercessory pleading, you become a great delight to God. It makes you greatly desired by God. It makes you like David, a person after God's own heart (Acts 13:22).

Invest yourself for God so that you become very precious to Him, one of His "personal treasures" (Mal. 3:17). Your whole-souled consecration, devotion to God, and investment of your time, your love and your possessions, indeed your very self, make you especially beloved and treasured by God (Deut. 7:6). As you thus delight in the Lord, He will delight in you (Deut. 30:6, 9–10; Ps. 147:11; 149:4; Zeph. 3:17), and you will become rich with God's special favor and love.

Life is given you by God for investment. The more you invest yourself for God, the more you are compounding eternal investments of God's future love and kindness, which He will lavish on you in heaven (Eph. 2:7). God has great plans to reward such spiritual investment. You can become an eternal billionaire in blessings.

What a fool you would be to neglect your eternal investment opportunities, which God is giving you now each day. Do you have eyes to see them? Don't make the tragic mistake of overlooking them. Invest for eternity now. Seize every precious opportunity to invest in God's eternal plans. Every day you can invest more and more for eternity.

Measure your life—not by man's measurements but by God's measurements. Measure your life by your eternal investments. You can't afford to neglect them. For God's sake, for His kingdom's sake, invest, invest, and invest for eternity.

Invest Your Life for God

Invest your time for eternity;
    Invest your life for the life to be.
Forever gone are the hours you've lost.
    Don't waste your life; count again the cost!

Your money place in the Savior's hand;
    It's only safe when on heaven's strand.
You never lose what you give to God,
    But lose all else when beneath the sod.

Invest your work in the Savior's plan;
    Work hard for God and His will for man.
Don't count the hours that you toil and plod—
    You'll reap again all you do for God.

Don't waste your life for a passing joy;
    Don't sell your soul for a fragile toy!
Give till it hurts; give your very blood—
    You live but once; live all out for God.

Wesley Duewel

16

MEASURE YOUR LIFE
BY ITS WORLD DIMENSION

G od so loved the world" that He planned for all humankind, gave His Son to die for all the people of all the earth, and today waits for the people of the world to come to Him for salvation. John 3:16 assures us of God's worldwide love. Jesus gave Himself for the life of the world (John 6:33). He is the light of the world (John 8:12).

LOVE FOR THE WHOLE WORLD

If your love is less than a world love, you are an ungrateful and unworthy child of God. If your love does not include many nations, if your prayer does not reach out across the earth each day, you are an unfaithful prayer partner with Jesus. If your spiritual life does not have a world dimension, you are a disappointing follower of Jesus.

World missions is not a minor activity of a few specially chosen people of Christ's church. It is a priority assignment to the whole church. Christ emphasized our going to the world more than our coming to church. If you stand at the judgment seat of Christ and have not had a world dimension to your life, you will be ashamed even though you know you are saved by God's grace. God's goodness to you will make you all the more ashamed that your responding love has been so narrow, so blind, and that you have not loved the world as He commanded.

If you are going to love the world as God commanded, you must do it now. After death it will be too late. If you are going to obey Christ's command to reach the world, which He gave to all of His followers, if you are going to add a world dimension to your prayer and investments, you must do it now.

If you have been failing God up to now, do all you can to make up for lost time. God expects every Christian to be a world Christian, to have a world love, to be involved in specific intercession for the world. Measure your obedience or failure thus far in investing your heart and life in God's whole world.

Undoubtedly Jesus taught many of His truths repeatedly as He sought to prepare His disciples and us for this time when He is absent from us. John's gospel shows us how He crowded into His last hours some of His deepest and most wonderful teachings on prayer, the Holy Spirit, and His will for us. All four gospels and the book of Acts show how two great priorities were on His mind in the last days and last moments before He ascended into heaven.

First, He emphasized the absolute necessity of His followers being clothed (Luke 24:48), empowered (Luke 24:48; Acts 1:8), and filled with His Spirit so that they could be and do all that Jesus desired of them as His representatives. The task He committed to them was too great for them without divine equipping.

Second, He emphasized the absolute priority of reaching the whole world with the salvation He had just provided on the cross. Their witness and assignment had a worldwide dimension. They were to reach all nations (Matt. 28:19; Luke 24:47), all the world (Mark 16:15), to the very ends of the earth (Acts 1:8).

Those two priorities are Jesus' priorities until He comes again. Our mandate is age-long. Our commission is unchanging. You and I were addressed in what He said to His disciples (Acts 2:39). You and I are responsible to be Spirit-filled and Spirit-empowered to fulfill His mandate for us. You and I are to keep up His priority assignment till every person in every nation has a fair chance to understand the Gospel and be saved.

Do you live with continual awareness that these two priorities are for you? Do you feel the hurt in the heart of Jesus that we have not taken His mandate more seriously? Do you believe it pains Jesus that perhaps one-fourth of the world has not yet heard the name of Jesus or heard enough about Him to understand who He is? Do you recognize that you bear part of the responsibility before God to see that the unreached have a chance to be saved?

Paul asks us unanswerable questions: " 'Everyone who calls on the name of the Lord will be saved.' How, then, can they call on the one they have not believed in? And how can they believe in the one of whom they have not heard?" (Rom. 10:13–14). Every Christian, you and I, are called to complete the unfinished task of world evangelization. Mission involvement is not optional for any true Christian. No one is excused from either praying or giving that the world may be reached. Christ finished paying the price of redemption, but the price of making that redemption available to all people must still be paid by you and me.

LOVE FOR ALL KINDS OF PEOPLE

We must have not only a heart that overflows with love. We must make love specific. God measures your love by the extent to which it includes all kinds and types of people. Do you frequently feel a real love for the prisoner? For the orphan? For the bereaved? For the sick? For the children of the world? For college youth? For the aged? You may have a special focus of love for any one of these. But your love should also include many different groups. Does your love go out to people of all occupations until you pray individually for sailors, miners, teachers, doctors, housewives, farmers, ministers? Do you love the police whom you meet, shopkeepers who serve you, those who serve you in other ways?

Your love must also embrace people of all nations. When God measures your love by these, are there any groups of whom you have almost never thought, for whom you have never prayed? How great is your love for Tibetans, for Chinese, for Nepalese, for unreached people of Afghanistan, of Mexico, Colombia, Peru, Russia, Poland, Germany? Does your heart rise instantly in prayer when you hear of earthquake, flood, riot, suffering in any part of the world? Measure your life by the world-wideness of your love.

When the Holy Spirit cleansed and burned the doubting out of the apostle Thomas by the fire of Pentecost, his devotion to Jesus expressed itself in a missionary heart. When the Holy Spirit cleanses and fills, He often takes our previous weakest point and makes it our strength in Him. Thomas became perhaps the most zealous, fearless, and active apostle, apart from Paul.

Thomas, in his missionary endeavor, started east. Both Eusebius and Jerome, early church Fathers, mention Thomas' missionary activity, which took him across

Parthia and Persia, and probably to India. Using the national names current today, Thomas seems to have crossed Syria, Iraq, Iran, southern Russia, Afghanistan, Pakistan, and India!

Ancient churches in South India claim Thomas as their founder. And to this day there is no more common Christian name in the southern Indian state of Kerala than Thomas. Tradition points to the hillside in Madras, South India, where, facing toward China as he was praying, he was martyred for Christ. The world dimension of Thomas' heart took him eastward as far as India and the Bay of Bengal of the Indian Ocean. The world dimension of Paul's heart took him westward, perhaps as far as Spain and the Atlantic Ocean.

Measure your life by your personal obedience to Christ's Great Commission, the evangelizing of the unreached of the world. Measure your life by the number of people who will be in heaven because of your obedience to Christ. Measure your life by its worldwide dimension of your obedience.

Is Christ satisfied by your involvement in His missionary mandate? Is He satisfied with your prayer life for the unsaved world? Measure your life by the number of nations for which you pray daily. Measure your life by the earnestness with which you pray for at least one or more of earth's mission fields each day.

You and I may be limited in our personal travel in our obedience to Christ. But there are other ways we can express the worldwide dimension of our heart. William Carey began that world dimension of his obedience when he was a young man supporting himself in the ministry of a small English church by making shoes. He put a map of the world on the wall before his cobbler's bench. He was too poor to buy one, so he made his own, pasting sheets of paper together. He drew the outline of each nation, and inside the boundaries he wrote the name, population, size, religion, and any other major facts that he could find about each nation. Then as he cobbled shoes, he prayed around the world. God made him, in time, the founder of modern missions, and though he served in the Calcutta area of India, he supervised and edited translations of the Bible in thirty-six different languages. Because he invested his heart in wide dimensions, God gave the shoemaker a ministry of worldwide dimensions.

Charles Cowman was known as the missionary with the map. Not only were maps on the walls of his office, as he spoke in missionary services he cited locations on a map. He prayed for nation after nation, and at times he would say, as he pointed to the map, "One day we will touch that nation." He believed for tremendous outreach, and though OMS had entered only Japan and Korea before he died in 1924, he had been saturating China with prayer for nearly twenty years. Today OMS is in fifteen nations. Many OMS leaders over the years have had maps of the world on their office walls or in their prayer rooms. You, too, can increase the world dimension of your prayer life by the use of maps. Will you do it?

In my early years in India, I prayed over the map of India, naming city after city, believing for souls. Later, when I understood better the immensity and diversity of India, I was almost embarrassed by the naïveté of my faith as a new missionary. I then concentrated prayer more on the area where we were working. Now, after fifty years, to my joy God has "exploded" the OMS work, and one by one we have been planting churches in those cities for which I had prayed so many years ago. God had not forgotten those prayers. Today I pray for dozens of cities and towns around the world. I want to inherit the promise of Psalm 2:8.

Are you a student, housewife, pastor, or layman?

Whatever your vocation, if your love is that broad, you can have a worldwide dimension of your life through prayer, through selective missionary giving. If your heart is big enough, you can find a way to stretch it to include the whole world.

The Lord's decree to Jesus was "ask of me, and I will make the nations your inheritance" (Ps. 2:8). Today that responsibility of asking is to be fulfilled by you and me as representatives of Christ. For which nations do you regularly ask? Let me suggest how you can be more faithful in your asking:

1. Place at least three other nations on your prayer list and ask for them daily.
2. Pray daily by name for at least one leader of each of those nations.
3. Pray daily for the revival of the church in those nations.
4. Pray daily for God to bless and increase evangelization and to raise up more gospel workers in those nations (Matt. 9:37–38).
5. Pray for liberty for the Gospel in those nations, and ask for God to multiply the harvest there.
6. Pray for whatever Christian witnesses and organizations have ministry in those countries.
7. Pray for God's mercy and blessing for all the people of those nations.
8. Pray for the unreached people and groups in those nations.

The more you pray for the nations God places on your heart, the deeper will become your hunger for their salvation. The Holy Spirit will give you that hunger. Learn all you can about the countries and people you are praying for, and pray for any needs you learn about. Measure the world dimension of your prayer life by the love Jesus gives you for those nations.

Measure your missionary involvement by the number of missionaries, pastors, or evangelists from other nations on your daily prayer list. Most missionaries will gladly give you a prayer card with their photo on it to enable you to visualize them as you pray for them. You may want to place a map of the world or of the nations you are specially praying for on your wall or in your prayer notebook. You can pray city by city for the larger cities there.

Measure your world love by your willingness to fast occasionally as you pray for the nations on your special prayer list. Measure your love by your willingness to have an additional list of names of nations, unreached groups of people, religions, missionaries, ministries, and other items for which you plan to pray as often as possible. You can choose them from as many nations as you desire, and then cover more and more of the world with your loving prayer.

Measure the world dimension of your life by your financial involvement in getting the Gospel to the unreached. How often do you deny yourself or make a special love gift for world evangelization? I hope that your church will be actively supporting evangelism in one or more nations. Become involved through your financial giving. You may learn of other missionary organizations that are actively involved in evangelism and in training evangelists. God may lead you to pray additionally for them and to support them financially.

You may find it helpful to correspond from time to time with missionaries you are supporting. You may find other ways to deepen your love—by exchanging family photographs, Christmas or birthday cards. Personalize your love in any way you can.

Measure your life by the developing love God gives you for the nations for whom you concentrate prayer.

Measure your life by your willingness to set apart time to pray for missionary outreach. Measure your life by the sacrifice you are willing to make for people in other parts of the world. Measure your life by your missionary involvement. Make your love a world love, your prayer a worldwide intercession, your financial giving a worldwide love offering to Christ. Be a world Christian.

All the World

All the world, all the world!
　Nothing less will do.
All the world, all the world!
　Share God's heart anew!
God's great task has but begun;
　Millions must be sought and won.
Reach your love to ev'ryone
　In the whole wide world.

Listen to God's holy call
　Echoing anew.
God needs you; He needs your all!
　Nothing less will do.
Ev'ry nation we must reach;
　All Christ's gospel we must preach.
There's a call and plan for each;
　Can God count on you?

Let man's need your own heart break;
　Let God help you see.
Some new steps you too must take;
　Look to Calvary.
At the feet of Jesus fall;
　Give your life, your soul, your all!
You can know God's will and call;
　Seek it constantly.

God has tears for you to weep,
　Prayers for you to pray.
God has souls for you to reap;
　God needs you today.
You are in God's worldwide plan;
　God through you must seek for man.
Will you pay the price you can?
　Yield your all this day.

Wesley Duewel

17

MEASURE YOUR LIFE
BY SACRIFICE

How different are the measures God applies to us from those we so often apply to ourselves! Sacrifice is one of the measures God uses continually as He evaluates our lives. Measure your life by sacrifice.

Beware how you measure the sacrifice of others. Sacrifice begins in the unseen realms of the heart, where none but God can see. True, it is manifest in many aspects of your life, but it is the thing easiest to misjudge. The deepest sacrifices are often not in the things most obvious to the human eye. Measure your own sacrifice, but let God measure the sacrifice of others.

Paul urges the role of sacrificial living as a part of our spiritual lifestyle. His illustration of sacrifice is something that perhaps would speak more loudly to a Jew in his day than it speaks to us today. Every Jew had experienced the presentation of a sacrifice in the temple. He knew it meant death for the animal that was totally devoted for the purpose of being offered in death as a sacrifice. Now we are to present our bodies (undoubtedly including our whole selves) as a living sacrifice. We are to be as totally committed to God to live for Him as the offering of a sacrificial animal was committed to death. The difference, of course, is that we *offer ourselves freely* while the animal was offered by another in the worshiper's stead.

". . . I urge you . . . in view of God's mercy, to offer your bodies as living sacrifices, holy and pleasing to God—this is your spiritual act of worship" (Rom. 12:1). Note the wealth of meaning in this verse:

1. You are a debtor to God for His mercy in providing salvation at the cost of the death of Jesus Christ His Son. You are a debtor for a host of subsequent mercies. It is in the light of this tremendous debt that you are to make a total love commitment to God—a commitment that is a sacrifice, a commitment regardless of the cost.

2. Your commitment must be voluntary. You freely offer yourself because of all God through Christ has done for you.

3. Your commitment is motivated by love because of God's mercy. Love rejoices to sacrifice for the one loved.

4. Your commitment is to be as a whole burnt offering, holy and whole—totally dedicated and consecrated to God, totally surrendered whatever the cost to you. You owe God no less than your all.

5. Your commitment and your living out of its loving implications is your spiritual worship. The word "spiritual" can also be translated "rational" and has something of the meaning of both in it. Rationally, intellectually, you can do no less in view of how Christ gave Himself for you. It is worship to love God this much, to make such a total commitment of yourself and your all.

6. The word "offer" or "present" is in the aorist in Greek. Grammatically, this means that it is a decisive, momentary act with a permanent result. This is not a tentative consecration of self. It is an act that has an

intentional finality about it and that determines your spiritual lifestyle from then on. You are not continually sacrificing yourself, but you are living in an attitude of permanent commitment, ready to make personal sacrifice whenever the Holy Spirit leads. It is a positive, dynamic commitment.

This attitude of sacrificial total commitment has practical applications in many ways. It may involve the giving of yourself in service, of your family, your time, your finance. It is an attitude of self-denial. It is taking up your cross. Jesus said, "If anyone would come after me, he must deny himself and take up his cross daily and follow me" (Luke 9:23).

Self-denial, another word for sacrifice, is a part of Christian discipleship. The disciple must be ready to follow whatever the cost. To take up a cross meant only one thing in New Testament times. The cross was the instrument of execution, and the person to be executed carried it. It was no ornament or romantic symbol. To take up your cross meant to be led to your execution.

Jesus was saying, "To be my disciple means to be willing to die for Me." Notice also that the cross is not placed upon you. You must voluntarily take it up yourself. This does not refer to sickness. You do not choose to be sick. It does not refer to an act that you are compelled to do. You must *choose* to stoop down, *voluntarily* take up your cross, and follow Jesus daily—even if it means great personal cost to you, even if it means risking your life for Jesus.

Today most Christians have a very cheap understanding of what it means to be a disciple. Today the average Christian lifestyle costs almost nothing. Jesus wants followers who are willing to volunteer to pay a price, to be willing to suffer, if need be, for Him. This is the holy commitment that He wants to characterize your spiritual lifestyle.

Measure your life by your willingness to deny yourself for Jesus' sake. Be watchful for opportunities to obey God and glorify God even when it is personally costly to you. Measure your life by your daily commitment to love, whatever the cost. Measure your love for Jesus by your willingness to suffer for Him, if the Spirit leads and God's cause and glory need this.

Measure your life by the number of times you deliberately choose to stoop to pick up a cross for which you qualify or of which you are capable and to bear this cross for Jesus' sake. Measure your life by your attitude of watchfulness, for opportunities to sacrifice for Jesus.

Sacrifice may or may not involve finances and material things. Your financial commitment is important to Christ. He is concerned about your giving. When in Jerusalem, He watched the gifts people gave for God's cause (Mark 12:41). He taught that tithing must be maintained, but that it also must be accompanied by a sacrificial spirit and by righteousness of life (Matt. 23:23). The tithe is never considered a gift to God. It is your debt to Him, and everyone who fails to pay his debt of tithe robs God (Mal. 3:8–9) and may be subject to God's curse. Does a partial "curse," at least a lack of great blessing, rest upon many Christians' lives because they are still robbing God? Sacrificial giving cannot be counted until after your debts to God are paid. Measure your life by your financial giving.

Measure your life by your self-denial in luxuries and comforts so that you will have more to give to extend Christ's kingdom. This is the area where you must be very careful in your judging. What is a luxury to me, may be a necessity to you in the place you live or the work you do. What is a luxury to a well person, may be a necessity to a sick or weak person. That which is a luxury to a parent may be a necessity to a child. Don't try to measure the self-denial of others. Measure your own.

The next time you are about to spend money for your clothes, your adornment, your home, ask God if He has a different suggestion for you. In the Bible, simplicity is always associated with godliness. Many things may not be sinful, yet may hinder a sacrificial spirit. Cleanliness, neatness, simple attractiveness strengthen our witness for God. But is there anything related to your personal attire, your habits, your recreation, your home about which God would like to whisper to you? Don't be too sure until you ask Him. Measure your life by your sacrificial lifestyle.

My parents were a godly example of a humble, simple lifestyle and sacrificial spirit for Jesus' sake. They spent as little as possible on personal needs. They ate simply, lived simply, and gave all they could to missions or to other outreach for God. I inherited almost nothing financially measurable, but a wealth of blessing and prayer.

Nine months after Charles Cowman was converted in 1893, he and his wife attended a missionary convention at Moody Bible Institute. Charles was deeply moved as the speaker, A. B. Simpson, founder of the Christian and Missionary Alliance, told of a young businessman and his wife going to Africa, trusting God for their support. Cowman had just been paid his month's salary and had it in his pocket. As the offering was taken, he took out his pocketbook and emptied it into the plate.

A little later in the service Dr. Simpson announced a second offering. Now what? Suddenly, Mr. Cowman took out his watch with its gold chain and held it in his hands. Then he looked in his wife's eyes and smiled. He looked down at her hand. She was puzzled. What did Charles mean? He looked up again in her eyes and smiled.

Then he looked again at her hand. Then she understood! Oh, no! she thought. But there he sat with his watch and chain in his hand. She took off her diamond engagement ring. And when the offering plate reached them, in went his watch and chain and her ring.

Sometime later, businessman Charles Cowman decided that month by month he would give all of his income to God except that which he needed for personal expenses. Then one day he said to his wife, "We have no children. We don't need the large beautiful home we live in. Let's rent it out to others and move to a small, simple apartment, and send the money we save to missions!" So they did.

It was that same spirit of sacrifice, that "all-for-Jesus" commitment, that in 1901 led the Cowmans to the mission field and to a lifelong sacrificial lifestyle. Not only did they live simply in order to give more; they lived without regard for their strength or health. Every spare moment was committed to the Lord—to praying, studying God's Word, witnessing, or doing whatever they could to advance the kingdom. It is not surprising that he won seventy-five of his telegraph operators to Christ in the first six months after his conversion. He formed them into the Telegraphers' Prayer Band. Later this became the Telegraphers' Mission Band. Today it has become OMS International. From that beginning on, OMS has advanced through the sacrifice of God's people.

Stanley Kresge and wife, Dorothy, have in recent years passed to their reward. Mr. Kresge, of Kresge stores and K Mart, was a Christian who carried his Bible with him. Not only have many Christian colleges and seminaries received large grants for the construction of buildings from the Kresge Foundation, but dozens of other colleges and universities have received sizable grants for building construction. In addition to the millions given by his foundation, he gave generously from his personal funds, as I am personally aware.

How did the Kresges have such money to give? By living frugally in their modest rural Troy, Michigan, home. Mrs. Kresge did her own housekeeping and cooking and was heart and soul with her husband. They kept a simple lifestyle and drove older model cars. After one of their trips home from Asbury College, Stanley wrote that they had a good 400-mile trip, with Dorothy doing most of the driving.

Mr. Kresge was frugal in expenditures on his personal clothing. They were frugal in their home. One of our missionaries, who stayed overnight in the Kresge home on several occasions, told of sitting at the breakfast table and watching Mrs. Kresge wrestling with an old toaster that was refusing to pop up. She kept banging it on the side, trying to get it to work. He said to me, "In my mind's eye I could see all those rows of shiny new toasters in K Mart stores across the country, but here she was using her old worn-out one." But that frugal spirit is why they had so much money to give.

The Kresges did not spend excessively on travel. When I was with him at the dedication of the Kresge Administration and Classroom Building at our Seoul Theological Seminary, it was the first time he had ever been overseas. He traveled simply, with not even a suitcase for his belongings. When asked to make the dedicatory address, he rose to his feet, held his hands toward heaven, and said simply but joyously, "Praise God from whom all blessings flow," and sat down. But the 1,800 students enrolled in our seminary, all of whom are preparing for God's work, thank God for his gift. He never thought of himself as sacrificing, but thousands are being blessed because of his faithfulness.

R. Stanley Tam of Lima, Ohio, for years the vice

chairman of the board of OMS International, has honored God with sacrificial giving. He began as an almost penniless salesman, going door to door and town to town, at times having to pray in funds to pay for the gas to get back home again at night. Early in his business life he made God his senior partner and began to give God fifty-one percent of the profits. Step by step he and his wife, Juanita, prayed over decisions large and small. After much prayer, he deeded his company to the Lord by legal contract, and from then on has received only a salary as an employee of God's company. All profits go for evangelism, supporting nearly 150 church-planting teams on OMS fields. In addition, from his own salary, he generously supports his local church, his denomination, and other interests. He is in constant demand as a speaker to churches, businessmen's and mayor's prayer breakfasts, and is often counseling others on the phone. For several years he has averaged four souls a day won to Christ by his personal evangelism, meetings, literature, and use of the telephone.

The Tams still live modestly; he carries his lunch each day in a paper sack, works long hours, and he and his son-in-law do everything possible to save one more dollar for evangelism. When they moved to their new plant, they hired a truck and did their own moving. They worked late at night, often till midnight, for weeks installing all the new shelving themselves, doing all the painting themselves—all a part of their loving sacrifice to give more and more for Jesus. Only God has the complete record, but OMS knows of some nine hundred church congregations that have been planted and organized and of more than 200,000 new believers who are now members of OMS-related churches because of the Tams' sacrificial commitment, simple lifestyle, and the investment of time, love, and life for Jesus and souls.

Measure your life by your sacrificial use of time. Nothing is wasted more extravagantly than time. Where your heart is can be measured by the things that you find time for. Most people find time to do what they really want to do. If you really want to pray, you will take less time in casual social conversation, will fast a meal and use that time for prayer, will get up earlier, or will sacrifice time from something else. If you really want to study God's Word, you will take less time reading the newspaper or will cut time somewhere else. Are you willing to sacrifice the time and read five chapters a day, thus easily completely reading the Bible through from Genesis to Revelation every year? What you really delight to do, you will count no sacrifice in finding time for.

You can measure many other forms of sacrifice for Jesus' sake. You may need to sacrifice the friendship of some people in order to obey God's call. You may sacrifice fellowship with your family in order to serve God in a distant place. You may sacrifice rest in order to witness to someone, or to get up earlier in order to be able to pray at length for your church. You may sacrifice a person's good will in order to be faithful in warning him of his sin.

You may sacrifice your chances of promotion in order to stand up for what is right in the sight of God. You may sacrifice your own plans in order to do the will of God. You may sacrifice a high salary by remaining faithful to God's call. You may sacrifice time in wholesome recreation or hobby in order to put Christ and His kingdom first. Every choice carries with it an opportunity for sacrifice, and the choice you make will serve as a measure for your life.

Measure your life by how continually you deny yourself to please God. Measure your life by how totally you keep surrendering your own will to do the will of

God. Measure your life by how joyfully you deny yourself when you make sacrifices. Is sacrifice characteristic of your lifestyle? Is surrender to God's will habitual? Is putting God's interest ahead of your own and God's will instead of your own so constantly your choice that your whole life is a living sacrifice to God? This is the measure of your life that is precious in the sight of God.

Measure your life, not by how much you get, but how much you give. Measure your life by the extent to which you put God first, others second, and self last. Measure your life by the extent to which you sacrifice to put Christ's kingdom first (Matt. 6:33), by the joy with which you deny yourself for Jesus' sake. Measure your life by loving sacrifice.

What More Can You Do?

What more can you do for God and souls?
   Don't be distracted by earth's vain goals!
Don't give a portion and keep the rest;
   Give God your all; give your very best.

What more can you do to reach the lost?
   Do you dare shrink back from any cost?
What more can you do to reach lost man?
   Ask God that question time and again.

What more can you do to do God's will?
   Can you more fully His plan fulfill?
Can you more fully God's call obey?
   Oh, let the Lord have His perfect way!

What more can you do in pleading prayer?
   Can't you more burdens for others share?
Can't you love more till you pray with tears?
   Do you pray, fasting, till heaven hears?

What more can you do in sacrifice?
   What more can you give to pay souls' price?
What more can you give man's need to share?
   What more can you do Christ's cross to bear?

What more could Jesus have done for you?
   Lift up your eyes and the world need view.
Don't fail your Savior and His great plan.
   What more can you do for God and man?

Wesley Duewel

18

MEASURE YOUR LIFE
BY HOW YOU GLORIFY GOD

The great purpose of your life should be to glorify God and do His will. Everything in your life can be done with a desire to bring more glory to Him. The unspoken underlying guideline in your every choice can be, "What will bring the most glory to God?" Superficially considered, many things seem to be unrelated to God's glory. But always, at least indirectly or potentially, they can add to or detract from the glory of God.

The supreme passion of your soul will be either God or self. It is ever a question of God first or me first. The issue is this—"What does God desire most?" Not, "What do I desire, or what would be to my advantage?" If you seem to have no ruling passion in your life, then self is on your throne. But if the ruling passion of your entire life is to bring more honor to God, then all of living, every day of your life, holds potential glory to God.

God's glory imposes a discipline upon all of life. "What will bring most glory to God?" is the question you must constantly ask yourself. Keeping yourself and your clothing clean and neat, keeping your hair appropriately cared for, keeping your home and your car orderly, tidy, pleasing, and suitable—this all should be done for the glory of God.

There are a multitude of ways that you can bring more glory to God. Not only does the Bible outline some of the more obvious ways, but the Holy Spirit is given you to guide you daily in bringing glory to God. You need not be constantly in the public eye to bring God glory. You can impact your home and family, your workplace and fellow workers, your church or your community by the example of your whole-souled commitment to glorify the Lord. It can shine in all you are and in all you do.

Earl Rainey was a cashier in the main store in Troy, Missouri. The Spirit-filled life of this young man gave him a pleasant disposition and a smile for everyone. He was always cordial, always helpful. He died prematurely, and in the county paper the store where he was employed inserted a large ad. In bold type at the top was "Earl Rainey went to heaven." Then it continued, "You ask us how we know. He worked for us. He attended meetings at the T_____ H_____ Church and said he got converted. All we know is . . ." Then they described the beautiful life that he had lived. Earl Rainey had lived to the glory of God.

John Newton's godly widowed mother washed clothes for the glory of God and to put food on her table. John followed his father to sea but went from bad to worse. He went from one ship to another and was finally sold as a slave to a black woman on the coast of Africa and was fed on crumbs from her table and the fruit he stole at night. He had only one shirt to his name. He escaped, went to sea again, and became a pirate-slave trader.

All the time his mother took in laundry, and day after day her tears dropped into the wash water as she prayed hour after hour for God to save her wayward son. Year after year she prayed on. At last, he was converted and became one of London's most beloved and eminent ministers. The entire Christian world today sings his autobiographical hymn, "Amazing grace, how sweet the sound, that saved a wretch like me." No Christian leader ever lived more to the glory of God than did humble, unknown Mother Newton. Who will get the greater reward in heaven, John Newton or his mother? Anyone can live to the glory of God. You can.

Jesus expressed the passion that was in His soul: "Father, glorify your name!" (John 12:28). When did Jesus call out that prayer? He had just given the illustration that unless a kernel of wheat falls into the ground and dies it remains unfruitful, but if it dies it produces many seeds. He had just said that the man who loves his life will lose it, while the man who hates his life in this world will keep it. He had just added, "Whoever serves me must follow me." Then He remembered the tremendous cost it would involve for Him personally in following the Father's will, and He exclaimed: "Now my heart is troubled, and what shall I say? 'Father, save me from this hour'? No, it was for this very reason I came to this hour." Then He called out, "Father, glorify your name!" Instantly God answered from heaven, "I have glorified it, and will glorify it again."

God will glorify His name through your obedient following of Jesus. He will glorify His name through your being willing to be a seed falling into the ground and dying so that a harvest may be produced (John 12:23–24). He will glorify His name by your being willing to give a costly obedience of whatever it takes to see God's will accomplished. Measure your life by that kind of godly attitude, by your willingness to pay a price for Jesus' sake, by your willingness to put God's glory first in everything.

God will give no rewards for having the most opportunities but for doing most with the opportunities you have. The more opportunities God gives you, the more God will require of you (Luke 12:48). Use the opportunities you have, and God will trust you with more (Luke 19:24–26).

A Christian minister was speaking on the subject of full surrender and the possibilities of a holy life. He drew a picture of what a holy home life would be if everybody lived according to the Bible. At the close he made an appeal to people to make that full surrender and be filled with the Spirit. A woman in his audience turned to the woman by her side and said, "That is excellent preaching, but I wonder whether such a life is possible." The other woman smiled back at her. "Well, I know the preacher lives such a life," she said. "I happen to be his wife."

If your life is focused on God with all your heart and soul, then even the most mundane and ordinary aspects of living can be done for God's glory. Even eating properly, drinking healthfully, sleeping adequately, and exercising faithfully can be done to the glory of God (1 Cor. 10:31). Many forget that their bodies are not their own. They owe their bodies to God for long, faithful service. They owe to God doing whatever is best for their bodies to keep them in top physical health. You are commanded to honor God with your body (1 Cor. 6:20).

Measure your life by the thanksgiving that overflows into other hearts because of you (2 Cor. 4:15). The thankful attitude of soul that the Spirit wants to pour out from your life in constant expressions to God and to others can bring respect and glory to God. A thankful heart bubbling over in joy and gratitude to God is a vibrant, living testimony to God's goodness and faithfulness.

Fanny Crosby, blind from six weeks of age, brought

glory to God wherever she went. From girlhood on, she knew the Bible better than any other book. As a girl, she could repeat from memory the first five books of the Bible, the book of Ruth, most of the Psalms and Proverbs, the Song of Solomon, and almost all of the New Testament.

Blind Fanny recognized God's goodness in everything—in the flowers, the trees, the grasses as she touched them, in the songs of birds, in the rippling sound of little streams of water. She began to describe it all in poetry.

She made up her mind that she would never allow blindness to darken her life or make her complain. She had a happy heart, and she scattered sunshine wherever she went, thereby glorifying God. She refused to let anything trouble her, sadden her, or disturb her faith. She was a welcome visitor in any home. She memorized the eight thousand hymns which she wrote to the glory of God. She was such a blessing that she was invited to speak to many large audiences. At the age of 94, February 11, 1915, she seemed in good health, dictated a letter and wrote a new poem, and went to bed. Before morning she had slipped into heaven.

What Christian has not joined in glorifying God as he sang songs Fanny Crosby wrote: "Blessed Assurance," "Saved By Grace," "Safe in the Arms of Jesus," "To God Be the Glory," "Tell Me the Story of Jesus," and many, many more. How many thousands of people have surrendered their lives to Christ as they heard the hymns "Rescue the Perishing," "Pass Me Not, O Gentle Saviour," and "Jesus Is Tenderly Calling." Perhaps millions of Christians have shared their testimony as they sang her hymns "Never Give Up," "He Hideth My Soul," "All the Way My Saviour Leads Me," "Near the Cross," "Draw Me Nearer," and "Praise Him! Praise Him!"

Millions of lives are richer because blind Fanny Crosby brought glory to God.

Measure your life by the prayer answers you receive as you constantly pray with others and for others. We are to carry continually the burdens of others (Gal. 6:2). Prayer answers bring glory and honor to God (Ps. 50:15). They testify to God's greatness, sovereignty, power, wisdom, and love. They prove to the world that God is alive, is on the throne, that God is love, that God is concerned with our lives. Oh, the potential to bring glory to God by prayer answers! What a dimension this can give to your life! Mighty prevailing prayer makes you a coworker with God. It adds an eternal significance to your life. As you go about your daily activities, you can keep breathing intercessory prayers to God and can keep expressing your personal love to Jesus. What greater way is there for you to bring glory to God?

Measure your life by your good deeds, which bring glory to God. In your sanctified humility you hesitate to attribute glory to God from your deeds. But they have a great potential of glory for God. Jesus urged us, "Let your light shine before men, that they may see your good deeds and praise your Father in heaven" (Matt. 5:16). Peter urged, "Live such good lives among the pagans that . . . they may see your good deeds and glorify God on the day he visits us" (1 Peter 2:12).

This suggests an important truth. The prayers you pray, the blessings you bring to others, the witness of your life may not bring instant public glory to God. But all of these will register on the minds and consciences of even those most vocally opposed to you. Just as Paul could not escape his goading conscience that came when he witnessed Stephen's shining face and forgiving spirit even in death by martyrdom (Acts 7:59–60; 1 Cor. 15:9), even so unsaved people who opposed you will sooner or later—at the Judgment Day, if not before—confess your influence and the glory you brought to God by your faithfulness. Measure your life by the good deeds and blessings you bring to others.

You are created to bring glory to God (Isa. 43:7). The Holy Spirit indwells you, fills you, empowers you, and seals you so that His presence can mark you in a way that brings greater glory to God (Eph. 1:13–14). The desire of the Spirit is to make you a constant glory to God. He wants your life to be so outstandingly different from the world that you are sealed as God's own. Can the unsaved people recognize God's approval resting on you? God's seal of loving recognition upon you?

Measure your life by the spiritual fruit in your character that bring glory to God. These are the fruit that cause you to resemble Jesus (Phil. 1:11). We love to sing the chorus of T. M. Jones:

> Let the beauty of Jesus be seen in me,
> All His wonderful passion and purity;
> Oh, thou Spirit divine, all my nature refine
> Till the beauty of Jesus be seen in me.

Measure your life by the extent to which you have clothed yourself with the Lord Jesus Christ (Rom. 13:14). The more closely you walk with Jesus, the more Spirit-filled your whole being, the more Christlike you become. Paul urges, "Clothe yourselves with compassion, kindness, humility, gentleness and patience" (Col. 3:12). Christlike compassion, Christlike kindness, Christlike humility, Christlike gentleness and patience—these are the holy virtues that bring great glory to God.

These are the qualities that cause the body of Christians, Christ's church, to bring great glory to God (Eph. 3:21). The power of this collective witness of the church is potent, and a church filled with Christlike people has a profound effect on the community as its collective life of witness adds weight to the witness of each individual life. This is one of the many reasons why each Christian needs to become an active member of a God-glorifying local body of Christians. Measure your life by your active participation in the body of believers by your adding to the weight of the testimony of the local group as a group.

The witness of your life brings special glory to God if your holy character, your bearing, and your forbearing with others, your Christlike forgiveness of others, and your lack of carnal responses to others is contrasted with insults, antagonism, and persecution from those who oppose you and Christ.

At such a time "the Spirit of glory and of God rests on you" (1 Peter 4:14). As God blesses you in the midst of hatred, slander, hostility, and injustice, His beauty is seen in you. Then your light shines brighter and farther than at any other time. Then, above all other times, God's glory is manifest upon you and through you. Then God's glory rises upon you and appears in the sight of others (Isa. 60:2, NASB).

Measure your life by the glory you bring to God when the pressures of life beat upon you. Measure your life by the Christlikeness you manifest when overworked, when health becomes a problem, when circumstances seem to conspire against you, when you are tempest tossed and harassed. That is when God wants your spirituality to be brightest and most Christlike. That is when He wants to clothe you with holy calmness and persevering faith. That is when He wants you to glorify God with a song of praise. Then, if ever, the world hears your song, sees your Christlikeness, and recognizes that your spiritual paternity is from God.

Bring Honor to Christ

Bring honor to the Son of God,
    Who gave His all for you,
By helping all the world abroad
    See Jesus Christ anew.
Exalt Him by the words you speak,
    But do far more than this.
Reveal Him as the One you seek
    Above all human bliss.

Bring honor to the Son of love
    By love to others shown.
Man can't see Him enthroned above,
    But man your life has known.
May Christ's compassion, tenderness,
    And mercy crowd your life.
May His self-giving graciousness
    Through you heal hate and strife.

Bring honor to the King of kings
    By your own poise of soul.
Reveal the grace salvation brings,
    Each thought in His control.
Remember you're a child of God
    And live His triumph here—
You dare not merely toil and plod,
    A slave to doubt and fear.

Bring honor now to Jesus' name;
    Live worthy of His crown.
Let all you do enhance His fame
    And add to His renown.
Let all you do throughout your days
    Commend the Christ you love.
That man may swell His endless praise
    With angel hosts above.

Wesley Duewel

19

MEASURE YOUR LIFE
BY YOUR CRUCIFIXION

P robably you have never considered measuring your
life by your crucifixion. Only a Christian would
have some understanding of this term. Only a Spirit-filled
Christian sees the full glory of a crucified life and rejoices
in the spiritual reality of this deep spiritual experience.

What Christ did for us by His crucifixion, resurrection, ascension, and exaltation in objective fact, we
appropriate subjectively by our faith identification with
Him. What He provided for us we spiritually experience
in holy reality. By faith the merits of Christ's death
become my own. In a spiritually real sense, I died with
Christ when He in awesome reality died vicariously for
me.

"I have been crucified with Christ" (past perfect
tense in Greek—the completed act on the cross has
permanent results in me). I am now dead to the law, but
also my self today is a different self. I am resurrected with
Christ, and I live a new faith life in Christ (Gal. 2:20).

The Holy Spirit wants to make real within you what
Christ accomplished for you. The full effects of the cross
include peace and reconciliation for you (Col. 1:20, 22),

crucifixion of your old sinful nature (Gal. 5:24), and crucifixion of the world to you and you to the world (Gal. 6:14).

That life is greatest in the sight of God that is most dead to sin, self, and the world, and most alive to the Triune God—Father, Son, and Holy Spirit. The church is filled with many carnal Christians who are surprisingly dead to spiritual things and surprisingly alive to self and the world. The crucified life has little significance for them.

The most deadly enemy to an effective and truly spiritual Christian life is a carnal self-life. A self-filled Christian is the opposite of a Spirit-filled Christian. To be filled with the Spirit is the secret of spiritual success and growth. To be filled with self is the cause of spiritual defeat. There is no risen life in the Spirit until there is a crucifixion of the self-life. Until Christians know in their own experience the reality of Paul's words, "I have been crucified with Christ," they cannot know the reality of his words, "I no longer live, but Christ lives in me" (Gal. 2:20). The life filled with self is never a life filled with God. God's Spirit will not and cannot fill you until you are empty of sin and self. Most people are too filled with the world, too filled with proud self-sufficiency to be of much use to God.

God works through those who are crucified with Christ and filled with the Spirit. For forty-six years I knew and worked with Dr. Eugene Erny, who in 1949 succeeded Mrs. Charles Cowman as president of OMS International. We worked side by side in the heat, pressures, and onslaughts of Satan in the founding years of our work in India. I knew him in sickness and in health, in leadership and in retirement. He was unusually Spirit-guided, Spirit-anointed, decisive, and dynamic in his leadership. More than that, he was truly crucified, Spirit-filled, and holy in life.

In administration, Eugene was loving and considerate in his decisiveness. He did not avoid issues but was gentle, yet strong in his firmness, humble in his confrontation, and forgiving and redemptive in attitude. He was a strong leader, but he was crucified.

He was dead to slights, insults, or resentment. There was no carnal defensiveness. He did not take personal offense. His sensitivity was sanctified. He was crucified. He was not suspicious. He was not negative. He was thoroughly wholesome. He was crucified. He was dead to personal ambition, self-striving, or manipulation of others. He was dead to covetousness, pettiness, and envy. There was a godliness in his demeanor, a spiritual fullness in his personal life, a sweetness in his strengths. He was crucified.

Year after year Dr. Erny's message was the highlight of the OMS annual convention. Often the earlier parts of the service took longer than planned. He did not want the service to have an excessive length. Instead of a half hour for his message, he often had twenty minutes or less. I have seen him have only twelve minutes, or only eight minutes. But there was absolutely no reaction, no resentment. He could take the remaining moments, get right to the point in the first several sentences, and often the anointing and power of the Spirit was so strongly upon him that within moments the audience was gripped by the message. Every moment added to the impact, and before you realized it, he was ending with a passionate Spirit-anointed appeal. The long altar again and again was filled with people making new commitments to God. He was crucified, and the Spirit could use him mightily.

Measure your life by crucifixion, not by zeal. Zeal is not necessarily a sign of spirituality. It may be a proof of self. No one is more zealous than a deceived fanatic. There is an infinite difference between the zeal of the sinful nature and the passion born of the Holy Spirit. Self-born zeal is self-conscious. Passion for Christ and for souls is a consuming fire that so possesses the Spirit-filled Christian one is almost unaware of it. It is not the result of self-effort; it is the outpouring of the Spirit throughout the depths of the soul. Unfortunately, such passion is seldom manifest because it is so seldom present. It is seldom present because self is crucified in so few. Yet it cannot be hidden when a Christian is consumed by it.

Measure your life by crucifixion, by the deadness of your self-life. Self expresses itself in manifold ways. It has its own desires. It seeks its own will. It is self-sufficient rather than being utterly dependent upon the Holy Spirit. It is fearful when it should be bold. It is weak when it should be strong. It is utterly inconsistent. It is uncontrollable by self-effort (Rom. 8:7). The Bible offers but one way to victory over it—death. Why is so little servant leadership evident among evangelicals today? Because so few are crucified. Why do so many people become quickly corrupted by influence or authority? Because they are not crucified. Why does such limited ministry of the Spirit characterize so many? Because they have never been truly crucified.

There is no resurrection power until self is crucified, not merely potentially but in appropriated personal experience. One cannot experience fullness of the Spirit until self is crucified. Love is not made perfect until self is crucified (1 John 4:18). More abundant spiritual life does not come until self is crucified. Continuous triumph in Christ and continuous fragrance for Christ are only for the crucified (2 Cor. 2:14–15).

When George Müller, founder of the orphan homes of Bristol and often spoken of as the apostle of faith, was asked the secret of God's using him so mightily, he replied, "There was a day when I died." As he spoke this, Müller bent lower, until he almost touched the floor. He continued, "Died to George Müller, his opinions, preferences, tastes, and will; died to the world, its approval or censure; died to the approval or blame even of my brethren or friends; and, since then, I have studied only to show myself 'approved unto God'" (2 Tim. 2:15).

How could George Müller trust God day by day for the food and all the expenses of two thousand people without ever advertising, ever asking for financial assistance, or ever answering people when they asked what his needs were? How could he carry this constant pressure without any sense of strain, without any worry? Often his expenses were met one day at a time. He never had any reserve. Yet it was said that "the Twenty-Third Psalm was written in his face." The secret is that George Müller was crucified. Since he was truly crucified, the Holy Spirit could fill him and use him unreservedly.

Measure your life by your crucifixion as you pray about 1 Corinthians 13. An uncrucified life may speak strange and seemingly angelic tongues. Yet it will not always speak in love but will resound like a brass gong, lacking the sweet, tender tones of love. An uncrucified life may prophesy and have wonderful spiritual knowledge, but it will prove lacking in love. It may manifest miracle-working faith, but it will manifest self also. An uncrucified life shows its lack of love by the absence of longsuffering, by envy, by pride, by emotions and words unbecoming to Christ's name, by self-seeking, by suspicion of others, and hurt feelings. Measure your love by crucifixion, and then measure your crucifixion by the love of 1 Corinthians 13.

A peacock may be proud as long as it is alive, but a dead peacock is not proud. A lion may roar with anger while it is alive, but a dead lion never shows irritation and bad temper. A mule may be stubborn in insisting on its own way, but no dead mule insists on its own way. A cat may constantly get its feelings hurt, but no dead cat shows hurt feelings. An uncrucified life may show many carnal traits, but a crucified life shows the beauty of Jesus, the beauty of holiness.

Henry Suso, renowned German mystic, was born about 1300 A.D. He was powerfully converted at the age of eighteen. He walked with God. One of his books was *The Life of the Servant*. One day he heard a knock at his door. A strange woman holding a baby stood outside. She thrust the child into his arms, saying, "Here you have the fruit of your sin." Suso stood dumbfounded as the woman hastened away. He had never seen her before. He was innocent of the charge. Quickly the news spread through town that Suso was not the holy man that everybody thought he was. He was a hypocrite! He was a fraud! Suso was crushed. He groaned like a dying man.

How could he prove his innocence? What should he do? It seemed more than he could bear, but he called upon the Lord for strength. Again and again he cried to the Lord, "You know that I am innocent." The answer came back to him from God, "Do as I did; suffer for the sins of others and say nothing."

Suso picked up his cross and followed Jesus. He took the child and sweetly, humbly cared for it as if it were his own, never saying a word in self-defense. Years later the unknown woman returned and published Suso's innocence to everyone. Perhaps God used Suso all the more because he was so crucified with Christ that he no longer lived but Christ lived in him.

Measure your life by the crucifixion of the passions and desires (Greek: "strong desires") of your sinful nature (Gal. 5:24). Desires and passions can be holy or sinful.

Measure your crucifixion by your strong holy desires and your holy passions. Measure your life by your holy hunger for more of God, your hunger for God's Word, and your strong delight in reading and meditating upon it (Ps. 119:47–48, 72, 97, 103, 162). Measure your crucifixion by your hunger to spend time with Jesus in communing prayer, by your joy as you come to the place of prayer, by your strong prevailing in prayer.

Measure your crucifixion by your holy passion of love for Christ, by your passion for righteousness and holiness, and your utter abhorrence of sin. Measure your crucifixion by your passion of love for Christ's church, for your brothers and sisters in Christ as you love them sincerely and deeply from your heart (1 Peter 1:22). Measure your crucifixion by your passion for witnessing and soulwinning. Those are the holy desires and passions of those who are crucified with Christ.

Measure your crucifixion by the absence of unholy desires and passions. Let no impure desires ever pollute your walk with Jesus. Let no bitterness, resentment, or critical spirit (Heb. 12:15) hide in your heart and destroy the sweetness of your fellowship with Jesus and the joy of your fellowship with fellow Christians. Such attitudes are a sure evidence that you do not yet know full crucifixion.

Measure your crucifixion by your absence of anger and rage. Let no action or word of others light a flash of unholy fire in your heart. Be angry with no one but Satan and with nothing but sin. Even so-called righteous indignation, if you let it remain for hours, can blur or destroy your godliness, your sanctified sweetness, and your sense of the nearness of God's presence (Eph. 4:26). Measure your crucifixion by your loving, forebearing, forgiving temperament at all times.

Measure your life by how crucified the world is to you and how crucified you are to the world (Gal. 6:14).

Has the spirit of the world lost its grip on you? Has it lost its pull on your soul? Have the worldly attitudes, entertainments, and pleasures of the Christ-dishonoring world about you and its worldly people been so crucified that they no longer influence you? Are you truly free to love and serve God as you will?

Measure your crucifixion by your freedom from bondage to the opinions, fads, and trends of our secular age. Measure your crucifixion to the materialistic, luxury-loving desires, fashions, and expenditures of your friends and peers. Measure your crucifixion to the tyranny of television and its time-wasting, often morally tainted programs.

"Don't you know that friendship with the world is hatred toward God? Anyone who chooses to be a friend of the world becomes an enemy of God" (James 4:4). Measure your life by how worldly or how crucified your lifestyle is. "Do not love the world or anything in the world. If anyone loves the world, the love of the Father is not in him. For everything in the world—the cravings of sinful man, the lust of his eyes and the boasting of what he has and does—comes not from the Father but from the world" (1 John 2:15-16). Are you crucified to that world, and is it crucified to you (Gal. 6:14)?

Measure your life by crucifixion. Measure your life by deafness alike to praise and blame, by your blindness to the faults of others, by your lack of hurt feelings, by your deadness to the desires of the sinful nature, to the lust of the eyes, and to the pride of life (1 John 2:15-16). Measure your life by your deafness to self-will and your delight in the will of God, by your deadness to pride and your glorying in the Lord, by your deadness to love of the world and your constant yearning love for God and His kingdom. Measure your life by your forgetfulness of self and your eager seeking first God's kingdom and God's righteousness.

Would you really measure your life? Measure how dead it is to all of self, how deaf, how blind, how insensitive to all that is unspiritual. But measure it by how sensitive it is and how constantly it sees spiritual vision, hears the soft whisper of God, and by how constantly it feels the touch of the Holy Spirit. Measure your life by how alive you are to God and how dead you are to all else. Measure your life by crucifixion.

Give Me a Crucified Heart

Give me a heart that is crucified;
    Give me a heart that with You has died.
Give me a life that is one with God,
    Cleansed by the flow of Your precious blood.

Give me a heart that is dead to self,
    Dead to this world, to its pomp and wealth,
Dead to its pride, to its search for fame,
    Dead to attempts to exalt its name.

Hang my old nature upon Your cross
    Until earth's gain I can count as loss,
Till unto me all the world has died
    As I unto it am crucified.

Give me a crucified, humble mind,
    Tender, compassionate, meek, and kind.
Give me a crucified, yielded will
    Ready at once any call to fill.

May my affections be crucified,
    Perfect in love, though most sorely tried.
Nail all my being, yes, all of me
    Unto Your cross upon Calvary.

Lord, may Your death e'er in me prevail;
    Free not my self from the driven nail.
Keep me each moment, Lord, crucified,
    Nailed to Your cross by Your riven side.

Wesley Duewel

20

MEASURE YOUR LIFE
BY GOD'S SPIRIT WITHIN YOU

How difficult it is to measure your life as God measures it! Indeed, how can we measure the Spirit's presence within us, His filling us, and His using us? Yet the Bible clearly indicates that God does just that. Scripture testifies that certain people are filled with the Spirit, and we are commanded to be filled with the Spirit (Eph. 5:18). We are promised the same depth of spiritual experience that was available to the apostles at Pentecost (Acts 2:38–39). Dare you measure your life by how filled you are with God's Spirit?

You have probably known times when you were very conscious that God's hand was upon you, when His power was evident in your life and ministry. It was undeniable. This is not surprising because this is the dispensation of the Holy Spirit. He has come to be active on behalf of Christ, active in applying the redemption of Christ and the results of that redemption to us.

All spiritual life comes to us through the life-giving Spirit. To be born of God is to be born of the Spirit (John 3:3–8). There is no spiritual life to be measured until then. "If anyone does not have the Spirit of Christ, he does not

belong to Christ" (Rom. 8:9). However, although everyone who truly belongs to Christ has the Holy Spirit
within, some Christians are more marked by the Spirit's
presence than others.

Jesus came that we might have spiritual life and have
it to the full, or abundantly (John 10:10). The Holy Spirit
has been given to indwell us in all His fullness. His holy,
almighty personality longs to fill our finite personalities.

To make the Holy Spirit more understandable to us,
the Bible uses metaphors from the physical world. But we
must be aware of the limitations of all such analogies. The
Spirit is *wind* (John 3:8; Acts 2:2), for He is invisible,
refreshing, and powerful. He is *water* in its various forms.
He comes to us as refreshing dew (Ps. 133:3; Hosea 14:5),
as a spring within us (John 4:14), as streams of blessing
within us (John 7:38), as rain showers (Hosea 10:12). He is
anointing oil (Ps. 23:5) and *fire* that cleanses (Isa. 6:6–7;
Matt. 3:11).

These are only helpful illustrations that symbolize
some aspects of the Spirit's work in and relationship to us.
He Himself is a holy, loving Person—the blessed third
person of the Trinity. He silently refreshes you like dew.
He springs up within you in blessings like a fountain or
spring. He flows from within you like a river of blessing.
He sets you apart by His anointing, as prophets were set
apart in the Old Testament. He cleanses you through and
through with His holy fire (1 Thess. 5:23) and burns
within you with a holy passion of love and zeal. He does
all this beautifully and thrillingly.

But the greatest reality of all is that He is your holy
indwelling Companion, Counselor, Guide, Helper, and
Lord. He applies all of Christ's redeeming grace to your
heart, equips you for holy living and service, and
empowers you for holy living and dynamic service and
for spiritual warfare for God.

Just as your spirit indwells your body invisibly but expresses itself dynamically through your body, so the Holy Spirit indwells your spirit, companions with your spirit, cleanses your spirit, empowers your spirit, and makes you spiritually fruitful. His inner working in your character produces in your personality the fruit of the Spirit (Gal. 5:22–23). These are godly qualities manifested within and then through you by His holy divine working.

When the Holy Spirit enters your life, He gives you spiritual birth, spiritual life. He adopts you into God's family (Rom. 8:15) and baptizes you into the church, the body of Christ (1 Cor. 12:13). He then witnesses to your salvation (Rom. 8:16; 1 John 5:6, 10).

When you as a believer yield your all in total consecration, the Spirit cleanses and sanctifies (John 17:17; Acts 15:8–9; 2 Thess. 2:13) and fills you (Acts 2:4, 39; Eph. 5:18). The Spirit is now able to exercise His holy lordship within your whole being, making you victorious, and empowering and using you as you serve Christ (Luke 24:49; Acts 1:8).

The Spirit is then at liberty to multiply in you in holy profusion that Christlikeness that is described as the beautiful Christly fruit of the Spirit (Rom. 8:23; Gal. 5:22–23). He does this to make you more and more like Jesus. Possessing your yielded self so fully, He does His divine work from within you. He will guide you (Rom. 8:14; Isa. 58:11), for He is your Counselor (John 14:26). He will guide and empower your prayer (Rom. 8:26–27). He will be your mighty Helper (John 14:26—"helper" is one of the meanings of the Greek word *parakletos*). He will anoint you (2 Cor. 1:21–22; 1 John 2:20, 27).

This is your great privilege as a child of God—to be indwelt, filled, and empowered by the Holy Spirit Himself. Once having made the total surrender which enables Him to cleanse and fill you, you can be refilled again and again as you live under His lordship and serve Him. Ask and you will receive (Luke 11:13).

Measure your life, evaluate your life. How fully are you living up to your calling? Jesus gives His Spirit to sanctify you through and through (1 Thess. 5:23–24). How fully have you availed yourself of His cleansing?

Many hymns have sought to express this blessed reality. Charles Wesley wrote:

> Oh, that in me the sacred fire
>   Might now begin to glow;
> Burn up the dross of base desire,
>   And make the mountains flow.
>
> Refining fire, go through my heart,
>   Illuminate my soul;
> Scatter thy life through every part
>   And sanctify the whole.

Measure your life by the cleansing, burning fire of the Holy Spirit as He indwells you. Have you made the total surrender that makes it possible for Him to fill and cleanse you? Measure your life by the fullness of the Spirit within you. Is there only a minimum of the Spirit's presence and power manifest in your life? Is it a true witness to say that He fills you and floods you with His holy presence?

Anyone who is truly born of God can be filled with the Spirit—anyone, young or old, man or woman, housekeeper, manual laborer, office worker, or Christian worker. Measure your life by your fullness of the Spirit.

Catherine Booth, daughter of William and Catherine Booth, founders of the Salvation Army, was known as Katie in her youth. She loved Jesus from her childhood and as a child gathered little groups of children about her to tell them of Jesus' love. At the age of eleven, she began to teach a Sunday school class. When she was twelve she began children's meetings in her home. The children confessed their sins with tears and were beautifully saved. At thirteen she began active witness in the open-air meetings of the Army.

When she was sixteen, she held evangelistic campaigns in many parts of London, and at seventeen, went across England holding three- to four-week crusades in city after city. Often the largest buildings were crowded out. Hundreds were won to Christ. Again and again an unusual sense of the presence and power of God characterized her services. Multitudes of sinners from all walks of life were saved. Hundreds of Christians made a full surrender of their lives, often with tears, and were filled with the Spirit.

People were spellbound by this frail, Spirit-filled young girl with a voice so sweet, tender, yet forcible. Some said she looked like an angel. She was only a youth, but she was filled with the Spirit and used by the Spirit just as much as she was used in her famous leadership of The Salvation Army in Europe in later life, when she was known as *la maréchale*, the marshal.

Measure your life by the abundance of the fruit of the Spirit. Are all aspects of that fruit constantly present in your spiritual life? Love, joy, peace, patience, kindness, goodness, faithfulness, gentleness, self-control (Gal. 5:22–23)—are any of them embarrassingly absent in your personality?

Paul explains in the next verse that this is another way of describing the crucified life: "Those who belong to Christ Jesus have crucified the sinful nature with its passions and desires" (v. 24). Only the crucified nature can produce uninhibited fruit of the Spirit. Are you crucified? Then Paul sums it up by adding, "Since we live by the Spirit, let us keep in step with the Spirit" (v. 25). Yes, it is the Spirit who makes the crucified life real so that you can manifest the godly fruit of the Spirit and keep in step with Him.

The fullness of the Spirit refers to the Holy Spirit's fully expressing Himself within you, fully possessing you, and fully using you. The fruit of the Spirit is the manifestation of the fullness of His holiness and life within and through you. The Holy Spirit does not give you a quantity of joy like a special reservoir within your nature. He is the Spirit of joy, and He rejoices within you and through you. He does not give you a quantity of love, but He Himself is Love. He loves within you and through you as He fills you. He does not store within you a quantity of power. He is the Almighty One, and He manifests His holy power within your being as He strengthens you in holy living and in effective service. He does not give you a quantity of holiness. He is the Holy One, and the only holiness you ever have is that which results from His living within you and expressing His holy nature through you.

What does it mean, then, to be more or less filled with the Spirit? It means that the Holy Spirit has more or less liberty to express Himself within you because you are more or less yielded to Him. It means more or less of His life is experienced within you because you have more or less fully opened your heart to Him and obeyed Him. He lives His life within you to the extent that you yield to Him and cooperate. You can measure His indwelling within you in two ways—either by your response to Him or by His manifestation through you.

Frances Ridley Havergal was born of godly parents who set an example of prayer, Scripture reading, loving cheerfulness, and punctuality. She was a precocious child and at four could write well and read the Bible correctly. She began to write poetry at the age of seven. She received a clear assurance of salvation at the age of fourteen, "and earth and heaven seemed bright from that moment."

By the time she was twenty-two, Frances had memorized the entire New Testament, the Psalms, and Isaiah (her favorite book). Later she memorized the Minor Prophets. From childhood she had unusual musical talent. She could play much of Handel, Beethoven, and Mendelssohn without the score. She sang with philharmonic orchestras, but refused to sing anything but sacred music. She gave much time to studying and marking her Bible.

Frances was deeply and constantly loving Jesus, but all this time she kept longing for a deeper experience of heart holiness. "Oh, that He would indeed purify me and make me pure at any cost." "Oh, that He may make me a vessel sanctified and meet for the Master's use!" One day she suddenly realized in her soul the experience of the promise, "The blood of Jesus Christ His Son cleanseth us from all sin." She wrote, "Yes, it was on . . . December 2, 1873, I first saw clearly the blessedness of true consecration. I saw it as a flash of electric light and what you see you can never *unsee*. There must be full surrender before there can be full blessedness. God admits you by the one into the other. He Himself showed me this most clearly."

From that day on, in the words of V. Raymond Edman, then chancellor of Wheaton College, who described her experience, "There was the constant experiencing of the fruit of the Spirit. There was undiminished and unchanging love for her Savior and for others. There was the joy that 'lifted her whole life into sunshine, of which all she had previously experienced was but as pale as passing April gleams, compared with the fullness of summer glory.'"

The Holy Spirit made her a constant blessing as streams of blessing flowed from within her (John 7:38).

"All for Jesus" was her motto. Her writings are filled with expressions like "inexpressibly sweet," "such a glorious life," "fullness," "infinitely blessed," "isn't it grand," "I have not words to describe it," "God's will is delicious."

Although frail and often unable to attend conventions, she was constantly a blessing to others. She was always witnessing for Jesus—to family, friends, strangers, working girls, students in girls' schools, in village homes, in the laundry, in home meetings, and among the elite, wherever she found opportunity. She conducted church choirs and spoke in tent meetings. She wrote, "Be willing to do 'odds and ends' of work which the Savior puts before you."

She loved to teach Sunday school classes. She often sang in churches, hospitals, and other places. In one letter she wrote, "I have not ten minutes; fifteen to twenty letters to write every morning, proofs to correct, editors waiting for articles, poems and music I cannot touch, four Bible readings or classes weekly, many anxious ones waiting for help, a mission week coming, and other work after that. And my doctor says my physique is too weak."

She died at forty-two, having already impacted the world for God. From her Spirit-anointed pen came devotional books, many poems and hymns, such as "I Gave My Life for Thee," "Take My Life and Let It Be," "Like a River Glorious." In what blessed ways God can use any Spirit-filled life!

Measure your life by your response to the tender but mighty Spirit of God. Measure your life by your hunger for Him. Blessed are the hungry hearted, for they will be filled (Matt. 5:6; Isa. 55:1–2). The more you hunger the more He is able to fill you. Measure your life by how deeply and how constantly you hunger for more of the Spirit's presence and working, by how much you really thirst, yearn, and hunger for all of His will and all of His presence. Measure your life by how deeply your heart pants for Him (Ps. 42:1), by how all consuming your desire for Him is.

Measure your life by how fully you are yielded to the Spirit. He possesses you as fully as you permit Him. The more you yield, the more fully He can indwell you. Measure your life by how fully you maintain a spirit of absolute surrender, by how total and how constant your whole-souled consecration is. Measure your life by your joy in accepting all His will, by the depth of your hunger for His will rather than your own. Measure your life by your utter self-abandonment to Him.

Measure your life by the minuteness and constancy of your obedience to Him, by the instantaneousness of your obedience, by the joyfulness of your obedience. The Holy Spirit is given to those who obey Him (Acts 5:32), and the more you obey the more fully He indwells and works through you. Measure your fullness of the Spirit by your obedience.

Measure your life by the Spirit's manifestation within and through you. Measure it by how fully you share His humility. Do you really feel your nothingness? Or do you usually feel self-reliant? Measure it by His holiness—do you really experience the absence of carnal desires and emotions? Measure it by His love—do you really experience His love, or is it only nominal in you? Measure your life by how constantly the Spirit rejoices through you, by how deeply His compassion longs through you, by how patiently He endures through you.

Measure your life by how constantly He guides you—in your speech, in your prayer, in your witnessing and soulwinning, and in the large and small decisions of your daily living. Measure your life by how constantly He anoints your service, by His power in your praying, by His freshness and unction on your speaking and writing, by His conviction on the lives of others through your witnessing and messages, by His blessing upon all your activities.

Measure your life by the extent to which the Holy Spirit indwells you and manifests His life, His love, His purity, His radiance, and His power within you. Measure your life by the frequency and extent of His powerful hand upon you and His power working through you. Measure your life by the extent to which He fills and uses you.

It is not how much you do in self-effort, but how much He does within you and through you. This is the purpose for which you were created, for which you were redeemed, that God Himself might indwell you by His Spirit. Measure your life not by any cheap and trifling earthly measures, but by the indwelling of the Spirit of God within you.

More of the Holy Spirit

More, Holy Spirit, still more of You—
    This is my heart-cry each day anew!
More of Your presence indwelling me,
    More of Your beauty so all can see,
More of Your blessing in ev'ry way,
    More of Your guidance throughout each day!

More, ever more of Your holy pow'r,
    More, more of God ev'ry day and hour,
More of Your triumphant, holy might,
    Complete enduement by day and night,
More of Your fullness to me supply,
    More of Your Spirit—for You I cry!

More, ever more of Your Spirit's fire—
    Oh, Lord, You know all my deep desire!
More, ever more of Your glory show,
    More of Shekinah I long to know!
Seal all my ministry now I pray;
    Seal with Your glory my life today.

More, Blessed Spirit, I need You more—
    This is my deep heart-cry o'er and o'er!
Oh, Holy Spirit, fill me today;
    Come and descend on me as I pray!
I need Your fullness more than before;
    Fill, Blessed Spirit, fill more and more.

Wesley Duewel

21

MEASURE YOUR LIFE
BY YOUR VISION

Your life will be no greater than your vision. It is vision that awakens your sleeping powers, vision that transforms startling facts into a challenge. It is vision that galvanizes your potential into action, seizes you where you are, and propels you into a life of blessing and significance for God.

Without vision you are in danger of drifting with the current. Without vision you will not rouse your latent abilities into sanctified service for God and others. Without vision your life will not impact your world, you will never become the person God created you to be and saved you to be.

William Booth was converted at the age of fifteen, and within six hours he was going in and out of slum houses, witnessing to the poor. He worked from 7:00 A.M. till 7:00 P.M. and then found time to bless others after that. He would stand on a box in the most sinful section of Nottingham, England, and tell the simple story of Jesus to the motley crowds. Every spare hour he spent reading the Bible and books about or by Wesley, Whitefield, and Finney.

When Booth was twenty, he began to preach to the social outcasts in a neglected district of London. He wept for the drunkards and others enslaved by sin. God gave him such a vision for the poor and needy that after his marriage he dedicated himself, his wife, and children to the poor needy "and their hell." William Booth believed in holiness and helpfulness. His coworkers had a holiness service every Sunday morning and evangelistic service every Sunday evening and were out among the needy during the week. The vision that burned in his heart as a teenager still burned when he died at the age of eighty-three. "Promise me," he begged his son, "to care for the homeless." Then he added, "I am not thinking of this country only, but of the homeless in all lands."

Booth was true to his vision, and today The Salvation Army with its ministry of salvation and uplift ministers in 91 nations of the world. There are more than 25,000 Salvation Army officers (ordained ministers) serving in 125 languages. More than 500,000 children are enrolled in their Sunday schools. Over the years hundreds of thousands have been won to Christ and millions have been helped in their time of need. Booth caught a vision!

If a vision really grips you, you will never be the same. If your eyes catch a glimpse of the vision God has of what you could be a year from now, you will see a new meaning in your life. You will hear a new purpose calling you to new advance for God. You will see God unfold new dimensions for your life. You will see things you never realized before. You will see with new clarity the way to add eternal significance to your daily living.

God has an important vision for you. He has a new unfolding plan for you. Don't look at what you are today. Get a vision of the person God wants you to be tomorrow. Don't sigh that you are hemmed in by circumstances that prevent you from ever being much different from what you are today. Catch the vision that God has for you.

God's vision for you is designed for no one else but you. You are loved by God. You are valued by God. You are important to God. God sees the details of your life today. God sees the problems that you face. He knows your present situation more fully and in greater detail than you do. He also knows what you do not know—He knows the future. He knows what can be your tomorrow. He is planning new phases of your life that are possible for you. He plans to use your life to bless others, to fulfill His special role for you. God plans a new you, if you can glimpse the vision He has for you.

Ask Him to open your eyes to see what He sees. When the enemy armies during the night surrounded Dothan, the city where Elisha was staying, Elisha's servant awoke in the morning and cried in shock and fear, "What shall we do?" Elisha told him not to be afraid because "those who are with us are more than those who are with them."

Elisha prayed, "'O Lord, open his eyes so he may see.' Then the Lord opened the servant's eyes, and he looked and saw the hills full of horses and chariots of fire all around Elisha" (2 Kings 6:17–18). The servant had eyes to see only the visible. God opened his eyes to see the invisible resources, protection, and future God had planned. God delivered them before the battle even started.

God wants you to see beyond the visible. The stark reality of the visible before you may strike fear into your heart. But there is a greater reality—God. The visible may fill your horizon with duties, limitations, and problems. God wants to lift your horizon and show you new vistas of what He can do. He does not deny the facts of your present circumstances. He adds His new greater facts to bring you to His tomorrow.

None of us has a full vision of all God sees before us and for us. You don't need to see that in all its detail. You need to see God. You need to see God in all His sovereign power, in all His perfect knowledge of your today and your tomorrow. You need to see God prepared to work good out of all that now surrounds you or confronts you. You need to see that God has a thousand ways to bless you, to use you, and to open His way before you.

Our heavenly Father is never surprised. He is never without resources. He never experiences difficulty. God is never ultimately defeated. He can work out His purpose for you if you are totally committed to Him, if you fully trust Him, and if you constantly obey Him.

Get a vision of your God. God is God. Don't measure Him by your problems. Measure your problems by God. Don't measure Him by your present circumstances; measure your present in all its reality by God.

George Müller was led by the Spirit to make the glorifying of God the first and only passion of his life. Shortly after his conversion at the age of twenty-one, he was led to trust God for all of his financial needs. He longed for some visible way to demonstrate to the world that God has not changed, that God is real, and that God can meet every need.

In 1835, he felt that the best way to do this was to found an orphan home based on the principle that he would never ask a human being for funds or never let the public know what his needs were. He would visibly prove that God answers prayer. This was his vision.

Step by step Müller's faith increased, and God increased the fulfillment of his vision. He brought glory to God in many ways. He cared for over ten thousand orphans before he died, often having to trust God for one day's food at a time. At times he called his coworkers to prayer twice a day to "pray in" food for the next meal. Always the orphans had wholesome meals. Hundreds of times neither money nor food was available for the next meal, yet just in time God supplied in some amazing way. Only twice was the meal delayed, and each of those times it was only a half hour late.

A. T. Pierson spent a night with Mr. Müller, and just before they retired, Müller asked Dr. Pierson to join him in prayer because they had nothing on hand for the children's breakfast. Stores were already closed. In the middle of the night, God awakened a caring person who was able to make arrangements for the delivery of food the first thing in the morning. Two thousand orphans had their breakfast on time. Neither George Müller nor any of his staff spoke of the need to anyone. In fact, so much food arrived that they were well supplied for a month.

For the last 17 years of his life, after the age of 65, he felt called to an international ministry. He traveled over 200,000 miles, ministered in 42 nations, and spoke nearly 6000 times, preaching to some 3 million people. Müller circulated 2 million Bibles or Scripture portions, 3 million other books and tracts, and gave $1,300,000 to support missions, including support for 115 missionaries in various countries around the world. He never let his need be known to anyone but God, yet he prayed in $7,500,000 for God's work and an additional $400,000 that was given to him for his own personal use, which he then invested in God's work. He lived humbly and simply, and when he died the total value of all his possessions, including his books, was less than $800.

Müller's entire life was dedicated to fulfilling this one vision: To glorify God by demonstrating that God was alive. He said, "When thinking of any new undertaking, ask, 'Is this agreeable to the mind of God? Is this for His glory?' If it is not for His glory, it is not for your good, and you must have nothing to do with it. Mind that! Having settled that a certain course is for the glory of God, begin it in His name and continue it to the end. Undertake it in prayer and faith and never give up."

If God is for you, who can ultimately harm you? Who can destroy God's plan for you? No one but you yourself by your failing to respond to God or to follow God fully. The Bible cannot be more clear. If God is for you, who ultimately can succeed against you (Rom. 8:31)? If God is for you, resources are available to you that far exceed your needs, your problems, and your opponents.

Get a new vision of God. God is greater than His universe. God is its Creator. God is greater than any need, any circumstance; greater than any combination of forces or any combination of circumstances. God can set limits beyond which Satan cannot step. God can use His angels to assist you in ways of which you are not even aware (Heb. 1:14). God can control the forces of nature, for God is the Creator of nature.

Get a new vision of God's love for you. Although God loves the whole world, He loves you personally. He is your God. He wants to be your God in greater reality than ever before. God has only begun to show you the greatness of His wisdom, love, and power. Jesus died for you. He not only wants to be your Savior, He wants to go with you through your tomorrows. He is planning for your life and for your eternity. He wants to use you exactly where you are.

Are you fully surrendered to Him? Do you accept His will above your own will, even if you don't understand all that He is permitting in your life? Have you surrendered your will, your life, your family, your future, your plans, and your all into His loving hands? Then have you trusted Him to fill you with His Holy Spirit? If you have, your Spirit-filled life will be one of victory over any circumstance.

God fills you to cleanse you, empower you, bless you, guide you, and use you. Give yourself to God to let Him bless as many people as possible through your smile, your words, your kindness, your helpfulness, your witness, your love. Ask God to bless and use you every possible way. Watch for the small opportunities He gives you today. Use them to show your love to Jesus and to others.

God can give you eyes to see opportunities you never saw before, to see hurting people whom you can bless beyond anything you ever realized. Don't expect to be thanked. Jesus was rarely thanked. But love people for Jesus' sake. Let Him love through you. Get a new vision of how He can love His world through you.

Our Lord will give you a vision of ways your prayer can bless those about you, those you hear about, those in need. Multiply the moments throughout the day that you invest in prayer. Sacrifice moments from things you would enjoy but don't need to do and give them to Jesus in prayer for others. Tell Him all about their needs.

You can invest your prayer over your entire community, over the whole world. Every moment you invest in prayer is a moment of cooperation with Jesus as His prayer partner because He is on heaven's throne constantly interceding for others (Rom. 8:34).

Every moment you invest in prayer is a moment of time you have turned into eternal reward. Don't lose your moments or hours in things that have no true value, that are really lost time, that lose the eternal rewards God delights to give you if you will only invest them by prayer in His eternal kingdom. Learn to make your moments count for eternity.

We have now come full circle back to where we

started this book. God is constantly measuring your life. God is planning rewards for you infinitely beyond all you deserve, but the rewards for which you will qualify depend on how you invest yourself today. Measure your life by your vision of ways God can transmute your moments, your actions, your love, your prayer, and your obedience into eternal rewards. Measure your life by your vision of what the unendingness of eternity means, of how much more important eternity is as compared with time, of how much more important heaven is than earth.

Measure your life by your vision of how important people are to God, of how He longs to bless and save the people of the earth. Get a new vision of how God can take your life today and touch your world and all His world by your love and prayer.

Your life is given you as a trust from God. It is your great opportunity to invest for eternity. Much of your life and many opportunities are already past. Measure your life by your vision of how you can make each day count for God and for eternity. Measure your life by your vision and by how you follow your vision, by how you turn your vision into eternal reality and reward.

A few months after his conversion, Bill Bright attended a conference in Forest Home, out from Los Angeles. After Henrietta Mears gave a challenge the night of June 24, 1947, four young men came to her cabin. They were Richard C. Halverson (now chaplain of the U.S. Senate), Louis H. Evans, Jr. (for years afterward pastor of Hollywood Presbyterian Church), John L. Franck (long-time assistant to Miss Mears), and Bill Bright (who later founded Campus Crusade for Christ).

> [The men] prayed on into the late hours of the night, confessing sin, asking God for guidance, and seeking the reality and power of the Holy Spirit. There was much

weeping and crying out to the Lord. At times, no one prayed as God spoke to them.

Then the fire fell. However it can be explained, God answered their prayer with a vision. They saw before them the college campuses of the world, teeming with unsaved students, who held in their hands the power to change the world. . . . Miss Mears and the four young men went out into the early morning transformed, commissioned, and expendable. Theirs was a world to conquer for Christ.[1]

In 1953 I spotted Bill Bright in India and asked a friend who he was. I was told that he was a Los Angeles businessman seeking God's guidance. He had already founded Campus Crusade for Christ as a vehicle to reach the students of America. Now God was enlarging his vision to a whole world. Over the years since then, Bill Bright has been characterized by an ever-expanding vision and a constantly daring faith and obedience to each new glimpse of God's purpose for him and his organization. The prophet Joel had promised that after the Spirit is outpoured young men will see visions. This was fulfilled in Bill Bright. When he reports what God has done, the statistics are almost breathtaking. Yet his quiet, sanctified humility never boasts. God can keep trusting Bill with new miracle answers because he never touches God's glory.

By 1960, Campus Crusade staff numbered 109 and was not only on American campuses but in Korea and Pakistan. God gave them a miracle location in Arrowhead Springs, California, to enable greatly expanded ministry. They began training thousands of young people to be soulwinners. Bill says, "I believe there are three basic reasons why God has blessed the Campus Crusade ministry in such a phenomenal way: (1) dedication to exalting Jesus Christ and His cause in every circumstance;

(2) a strong emphasis on the ministry of the Holy Spirit in the life of the believer; and (3) special, detailed, comprehensive training for every staff member, student and layman in how to live holy lives and share their faith in Christ with others." Included in the ten basic training principles used for all their people and for those to whom they minister are training in how to be filled with the Holy Spirit, how to walk in the Spirit, how to witness in the Spirit, how to help fulfill the Great Commission.

Vision by vision this ministry has expanded to a Here's Life Campaign to reach the cities of America and later to many of the cities of the world. Explo '74 in Korea registered 320,000 people for a similar event. Innovative and ongoing ministries have been added one by one— high school evangelism, collegiate evangelism, prison and military evangelism, Athletes in Action, and Agape Ministries to believers around the world. A Christian embassy in Washington, D. C., ministers to diplomats and government officials from many nations in Washington and at the United Nations in New York. Millions of people have seen the *Jesus* film, which is based on the Gospel of Luke and includes nothing but the words of Scripture; thousands of those viewers have made a commitment to Christ. It has been translated into more than two hundred languages, and the ministry plans translations into a thousand other dialects.

More than 16,000 staff persons around the world now seek to fulfill the ever-expanding vision. The current major strategy is New Life 2000, by which Dr. Bright hopes to establish 5000 New Life training centers, have ministries on 8000 campuses around the world, and 5000 film teams showing the Jesus film continually. He prays to see a billion people won to Christ by the end of this century as they work together with Christians of many organizations.

Does this vision seem overwhelming? Remember, Bill Bright's vision has developed step by step. Each great vision must begin with a comparatively small vision, and then God can enlarge it step by step. Dr. Bright challenges each one to (1) think supernaturally, (2) pray supernaturally, (3) plan supernaturally, and (4) expect great things from God.

You are not Bill Bright, but God has a specific vision for you. Are you as faithful to God's vision for you as others are to their expanding vision? Get a vision of your family, your church, your community. Get God's vision for a whole world. Are you seeing your opportunities as God sees them? Are you seeing the world as God sees it? Pray God to open your eyes to the vision He has for you.

Don't lose your moments, hours, days, and years. Don't lose your life's great opportunities. Measure your life as God does. You cannot change your past. But from this day on, love your God with all your heart, with all your soul, with all your mind, and with all your strength (Mark 12:30). From this day on, love your neighbor as yourself (v. 31), love your world as God loves it. From this day on, make your life count for eternity, and measure your life in the light of eternity. Then great will be your reward. Throughout eternity you will thank God that you began to measure your life by His measures.

Note

[1]Ethel M. Baldwin and David V. Benson, *Henrietta Mears and How She Did It* (Glendale: Regal, n.d.), 232–33.

Give Me a Vision

Give me a vision of sin's dark night,
   Millions still fettered by Satan's night.
Show me the darkness where shines no light—
   Show me the need of the world.

Give me a vision of souls in need;
   Give me a vision of hearts that plead.
Burden me, Lord, till I intercede,
   Giving my all for the world.

Give me a vision of endless gloom,
   Millions who hasten to Christless doom.
Hell to receive them is making room
   For all the lost of the world.

Give me a vision of distant lands
   Lost without Christ, bound by Satan's bands.
Show me the millions with outstretched hands.
   Show me the whole wide world.

Show me the Christ of eternity;
   Show me Gethsemane's agony.
Show me the love of dark Calvary;
   Give me His love for the world.

Wesley Duewel

I Challenge You

I challenge you now at this crisis hour
    To take up your cross in the Savior's pow'r.
Oh, do something worthy for God and man—
    Come sacrifice all for the Savior's plan.

I challenge you now when the need is great;
    I challenge you now when the hour is late!
Remember how brief is your life's short span—
    Oh, do something worthy for God and man.

When you see the cross of the Son of God,
    When you see the martyrs who shed their blood,
When you o'er your record of living scan
    What have you ever suffered for God and man?

Do you really gladden your Savior's heart?
    Do you share His burden and do your part?
Do you prove to Him that your love is true?
    What price are you paying to give and do?

Come, do something worthy for Jesus now!
    Come finish your crown for His thorn-pierced brow.
Oh, shun not the cross, but complete His plan—
    It's now or it's never for God and man.

Wesley Duewel

If God has made this book a blessing to you and you wish to share a testimony, or if you wish the author to remember you in a moment of prayer, feel free to write:

Dr. Wesley L. Duewel
OMS International, Inc.
Box A
Greenwood, Indiana 46142-6599

INDEX OF POEMS

INDEX OF ILLUSTRATIONS

OTHER BOOKS
BY WESLEY DUEWEL

Touch the World Through Prayer. A challenging, readable manual on prayer that has been used by God to revitalize the prayer lives of thousands. A Christian best-seller.

Let God Guide You Daily. A manual on guidance to help you enter into the joy of God's guidance as the daily experience of your life.

Ablaze for God. A book to challenge all Christians, especially Christian workers and lay leaders, to a life and service Spirit-filled, Spirit-empowered, and mightily used by God.

Mighty Prevailing Prayer. Let the Spirit use this powerful volume to make your intercession mighty before God. A guide to intensified intercession and prayer warfare.

Some 320,000 copies of Dr. Duewel's books are in circulation. All are published by Zondervan Publishing House and are available at Christian bookstores everywhere.